Flicks&Clicks

How to create **websites** and **catalogues** that sell more

Mel Henson

Flicks & Clicks

How to create **websites** and **catalogues** that sell more

Foreword by Nigel Swabey

Flicks & Clicks - How to create **websites** and **catalogues** that sell more

First published in 2011 by
Ecademy Press
48 St Vincent Drive, St Albans, Herts, AL1 5SJ
info@ecademy-press.com
www.ecademy-press.com

Printed and bound by Lightning Source in the UK and USA
Designed by Michael Inns
Set in Trade Gothic and Warnock by Karen Gladwell

Printed on acid-free paper from managed forests. This book is
printed on demand, so no copies will be remaindered or pulped.

ISBN 978-1-907722-04-2

Contents

Dedication

For J, H & S.

If you've enjoyed Flicks and Clicks, then please

Follow **Flicks & Clicks** on twitter **@flicksandclicks**

Visit **www.wordsthatsell.co.uk** for updates and free downloads

Post a review on **www.amazon.co.uk**

Foreword

There's an old saying, 'Retail is Detail'. To that I would add that the key to success for anyone in e-commerce retailing is knowledge. Ever since I set up my first catalogue, Kaleidoscope, in 1974 I have felt that one of the main challenges facing this industry is a lack of educational resources. That's true when the economy is booming, and it's even more true when we're facing difficult financial times as we are today.

Industry-wide education is an issue that's particularly close to my heart, which is why, together with others, I founded the Catalogue Exchange. By sharing experiences, we all help each other to improve our businesses and avoid making repeated mistakes. However, the e-commerce industry has conspicuously lacked an authoritative book that covers the basics. Now at last we have a practical 'how-to' guide to planning and improving retail websites and mail order catalogues.

This book breaks down catalogues and websites into their individual elements and illustrates key points with real-life examples. You are taken through the journey of planning a catalogue and a website, from developing the pages through to how to write compelling sales copy. The mysteries of building a brand are unravelled and there are tips on finding consumer benefits. Finally we see how testing is the bedrock of ongoing success, with lots of ideas to try out in your own business.

As one of the UK's leading multichannel strategists and copywriters, with dozens of catalogues and websites to her credit, Mel Henson is ideally placed to write this book. With her background in classical direct marketing, she is always interested in results and has a particular passion to discover why some techniques bring in more sales than others.

More than that, she is always extremely generous with her knowledge, regularly running workshops to encourage others to learn the tricks of the trade. Anyone who has heard one of Mel's lively conference presentations goes away not just entertained but armed with a raft of techniques to put into practice.

That depth of knowledge and enthusiasm to share it shines through in this book. It's a joy to read, and useful advice leaps out from every page. When I was honoured with a lifetime achievement award by ECMOD in 2009 (www.ecmod360.co.uk), I said that I wished I could explain to retailers how important – and how easy – it is to create a catalogue that gets people queuing up and ready to place orders. With this book, Mel has done just that.

Whether you're a start up wanting to learn the basics, or an established retailer looking for information on best practice, Flicks and Clicks will help you master the art of creating profitable catalogues and websites, and give your multichannel business the competitive edge for years to come.

Nigel Swabey,
Chairman of Scotts & Co and President of Catalogue Exchange

Introduction

When I was about ten, my school decided to raise some funds by holding a second hand uniform sale. Outgrown kit could be labelled with the size, name, description and price and taken along to the school hall for a grand and glorious sale.

My mother said I could help with the labelling, so I was let loose with a felt tip pen and some sticky labels. On the first label I wrote "A stylish jumper with ribbed cuffs and stripe detail round the V-neck". This was followed with "A stunning pleated skirt in easy-care polyester. Excellent condition". It wasn't exactly what my mum had in mind, but they went in the sale anyway.

Copywriting that sells

Although I didn't know it at the time, this was my first attempt at commercial copywriting. At the sale the next day, we drew a small crowd. Everyone was picking up my labels and reading them out loud to their friends. Our little Tupperware box started to fill up with cash.

From that point on I was absolutely hooked. I loved the writing, I loved seeing people smile as they read the words and I loved seeing their faces light up as they went away clutching their new possessions. That passion is still with me today. Even now I get a real buzz every time I write a piece of copy and see the results.

When I left school I landed a job in an advertising agency by pretending I could type. (A skill I rapidly picked up to avoid being sacked.) In between making cups of tea and changing the toner on the photocopier, I got the chance to go along to photo shoots and recording sessions, which set me on the path to a career in advertising.

I studied marketing at evening classes and ended up at some of London's top ad agencies making TV and radio commercials for Carte D'Or Ice Cream, Immac (now Veet) and Melitta Coffee and rubbing shoulders with celebrities like Ruby Wax and Harrison Ford.

Direct marketing that makes a difference

But it was my experiences at Ogilvy & Mather Direct, the UK's largest direct marketing agency that proved the most valuable in the long run. The agency specialised in direct mail, and every element was tested and measured, from the copy and the offer right down to the colour of the envelope. It was there that I learned how simply changing a few words or moving a photograph could send sales shooting up.

When I turned freelance, some years later, I noticed that very few catalogues or e-commerce sites embraced classic direct marketing and branding techniques. I felt sure that applying some of these proven principles to catalogues would reap rewards, and when I found clients willing to experiment, my hunch proved right.

Spectacular results

Results were spectacular. Donald Russell, now Britain's leading gourmet food mail order firm, was the first to let me put theory into practice. Response rates for those early mailings were way above any industry averages.

Then I teamed up with Catalogues 4 Business, one of a handful of agencies specialising in catalogue design. The team there, led by Ian Simpson, designed to take advantage of eyeflow and hot-spots using hero shots, call-outs, pace, and other specialist techniques. The addition of direct marketing style copy proved to be a magic combination.

One of the first catalogues we worked on together – the childrenswear brand Muddy Puddles – doubled its sales with the first mailing. The next, for Turtle Mat, a designer doormat company, pulled in three times more sales than anything that had been mailed before.

As the internet took off, applying the same direct marketing principles to websites also proved a winning formula. After all, customers haven't changed, just because there's a new medium. They still buy in the same way.

At one time it was predicted that the internet would make catalogues extinct, but with hundreds being mailed out every month to millions of homes in the UK alone, they're clearly alive and well. Many e-commerce businesses have found that reaching customers with both a website and a catalogue is more effective than a website alone. Their experience is echoed by several independent studies proving that customers who receive a catalogue spend around 60% more online.

Sales trigger

The reason that catalogues are such a good trigger for web sales is because they go to the customer and demand attention, unlike websites which wait passively for the customer to come to them. Catalogues need no equipment and you can see the whole thing at a glance, whereas websites have to be viewed one page at a time.

That's why browsing a catalogue is also a popular leisure activity for all ages. In a recent survey by Verdict Consulting on behalf of Pindar, teenagers and grannies described putting their feet up on the sofa and relaxing with a cuppa to decide what to buy, then going online later to order. People even admit to reading catalogues in bed.

This cosy scenario is especially true for sectors like gifts and homewares. "Creating and distributing catalogues is the lifeblood of our business" says Dara O'Malley, Managing Director of House of Bath. "Our customers have told us that they really enjoy receiving our catalogues, browsing through them in their own time and finding new products that appeal to them. We know that most of our sales are spontaneous purchases that rely on the catalogue to create the customer need."

It's a sentiment echoed in the fashion industry too. Judith Pilkington, former CEO of upmarket Italian clothing retailer Artigiano says, "The catalogue is essential. People love them, just like they enjoy browsing through glossy fashion magazines". Johnnie Boden has two words to sum up why the Boden clothing catalogue is vital to his business, "The lavatory. People always underestimate how important that is."

Catalogues and websites

So until we all start taking our laptops into the loo, it looks as if catalogues are here to stay – and so too are websites. At the moment, most companies have separate online and offline marketing departments. However, each discipline has a lot to learn from the other as there are many techniques and tricks that cross over both print and cyberspace.

In the future, sharing this knowledge will become even more important as the division between online and offline marketing becomes eroded. Already, it's possible to print catalogues with bar codes that go straight through to the website. One day they could even be 'read' by a smart phone or one of the new breed of mobile devices and purchased in an instant. Dubbed m-commerce, it could herald an age where customers won't even have to leave the comfort of their sofa – or throne – to indulge in a little retail therapy.

It's a far cry from the day I took my first steps into direct marketing, standing behind a trestle table piled high with second hand uniform. Nowadays the felt tip pens and labels have been replaced with jazzy technology, gorgeous design and slick photography. Yet even so, many of the underlying principles of selling are still the same.

Flicks and clicks

Through working with some very talented clients and colleagues over the years, I've learned many secrets of successful online and offline marketing. I'm delighted to share them with you here and I hope they help you gain more flicks of your catalogues, more clicks on your website and more profits on your bottom line.

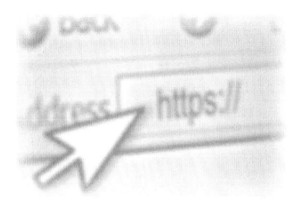

1 | Anatomy of a website

To understand how websites sell, it's useful to take a look at how they are made up. E-commerce sites are sometimes described as 'stores without walls' – a description that has also been applied to catalogues for decades. Both find ways to reproduce all the good things about going shopping in a bricks and mortar store. Shelf displays are replaced by gorgeous photos and instead of salespeople there is copy.

Like a shop, both catalogues and websites aim to attract as many people as possible, then funnel them towards making a purchase. Just as an enticing shop window draws people in, so too does the home page or catalogue front cover. Even the way catalogues and websites are arranged mimics the departments or sections of a store. They are all laid out to help people find what they are looking for and encourage them to explore further and discover new products they can't resist. When it's time to pay, a website has a checkout instead of till points and sales desks.

Many of the challenges that face a physical store also apply to websites - it's just the technology and some of the characteristics that are different. Dissecting the website into its different elements helps to show how each part functions and what makes a website an easy, enjoyable and trusted place to shop.

This chapter is not about all the ins and outs of building a website (a very different skill from designing website graphics or website architecture) nor the high-tech bells and whistles. Here are some broad-brush principles, and a few tips on the simple things that can make a big difference, with lots of ideas that you can put into practice on your own site and test out for yourself.

Parts of a website

The skeleton of a website is its navigational structure, which holds all the other parts of the site including:

- *Home page*
- *Category pages*
- *Product pages*
- *Static pages*
- *Landing pages*
- *Checkout*

Navigational structure

Navigation is so critical that it accounts for a staggering 40-60% of the success of your website, according to research by leading web usability firm Eight by Eight. If your visitor can't find something easily on your site, they assume you don't sell it, so it's important to get the structure right.

C-navigation

There are many ways to structure and lay out your site, but one of the most successful is C-navigation, so called because it resembles a 'C' shape.

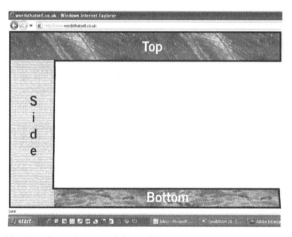

C-navigation with tabs along the top, side and bottom.

The right hand column doesn't form part of the navigation. For some reason people are simply not hard-wired to navigate from the right. When people click away from a site, the majority have their eyes on the right hand side. Therefore the right hand column is a good place to put things which might tempt the visitor to stay a little longer and not leave.

Users view websites in a **'dominant reading pattern'** that looks somewhat like an 'F' shape. Jakob Nielsen, one of the leading researchers in the field, has conducted hundreds of eye-tracking studies. He found that patterns vary from site to site and page to page, but generally users first read in a **horizontal movement**, usually across the upper part of the content area – the top stroke of the 'F'.

Next, users move down the page a little and then read across in a **second horizontal movement** that's typically shorter than the first sweep. This forms the second stroke of the 'F'.

Finally, users scan down the content's left side in a **vertical glance** which forms the stem of the 'F'. C-navigation mirrors this natural eyeflow, which is why it works so well.

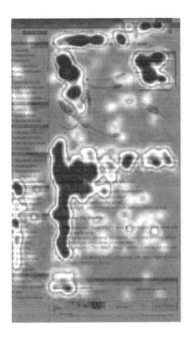

■ Heat maps reveal how people typically read web pages in an 'F' pattern. Reproduced from **http://www.useit.com/alertbox/reading_pattern.html.**

C-navigation – *top tiers*

The top part of the 'C' sometimes has two or three distinct tiers such as:

Top tier 1 - *Product tabs*. This has the effect of immediately telling visitors what you sell, as well as helping with the navigation. These tabs do not have to show the complete range of products, just the main product categories.

Top tier 2 – *Action bar.* This bar has tabs (usually five) that are all about the customer taking an action, such as 'Shop by Price', 'Request a Catalogue', 'Ask an Expert' or ' Recommend a Friend'. It should be kept clear of passive tabs such as 'About Us' which is something for the customer to look at, rather than something for them to do.

Top tier 3 – *Filters*. If it's appropriate, then the third tier may have an array of filters such as 'Shop by Price', 'Shop by Age', 'Shop by Occasion', 'Shop by Size' or whatever is relevant to the types of product on offer.

■ The UK's largest online gourmet foods company, **Donald Russell**, uses a 'C' shaped navigation system.

C-navigation – **side**

The left hand column of the 'C' is an index of the store showing product categories, listed in alphabetical order (rather than leading with the most popular products as on the top bar). Then come sections such as About Us, FAQs, Location/directions, Buyers Guides and Environmental Policy.

The very top of this column is a good place to put a 'request a catalogue' box and a newsletter sign-up to capture email addresses. You can ask for the sign-up more than once by adding a second box lower down, and using different wording. For example the first mention might say "Sign up for our e-newsletter" and the second could say "See our latest email special offer".

*C-navigation – **bottom***

According to studies, around 25% of people navigate websites from the bottom up, so some websites repeat the top navigation here. This decision is largely a matter of personal choice – and testing to find out what works for your site – as even the experts disagree about bottom navigation. Some believe it makes the site cluttered and bloated, while others claim that the 'redundancy' of matching graphics top and bottom makes people feel comfortable.

The bottom navigation is also the place for basic housekeeping and information that you are obliged to have but won't win you any sales. The majority of visitors either have no interest in your privacy policy or are so keen to see it they will make the effort to find it. The bottom of the page is where you can tuck non-selling elements neatly out of the way, including:

- *Site map*
- *Privacy policy*
- *Confidentiality*
- *Careers*
- *Environmental policy (if no room in the left hand navigation)*
- *Affiliates*
- *Company logo, address, phone number and email address*
- *Symbols for trade bodies and other memberships*
- *Symbols for ISO 9001, Investors in People and other certificates*
- *Any other small print*

Why use C-navigation?

There are sites that use other formats for navigation, but this 'C' structure is generally regarded as the easiest to use. When you have a clear navigation that helps visitors to find things rather than forcing them to go looking, you sell more. It also makes visitors feel comfortable and confident rather than being distracted or frustrated, so they stay on your site for longer and, as the saying goes, "The longer they stay, the more they pay".

Home Page

The first priority of a home page is to reach out to visitors and encourage them to want to stay and do something. The jargon for this is a 'conversion', which, to traditional catalogue marketers, means converting a prospect into a customer and making a sale. In web parlance, a conversion is simply any sort of specified action. This could be buying a product but is more likely to be steps on the way to buying such as signing up for a newsletter or clicking through to another page.

A welcoming website home page:

- *Makes it immediately clear what you are selling*
- *Is easy for visitors to find what they're looking for*
- *Looks fresh, seasonal and well-visited*
- *Looks trustworthy*
- *Gives potential shoppers reasons to buy from this site rather than another*
- *Invites visitors to look at the goods for sale*
- *Asks visitors for their email address – several times. (This is vital so that you can carry on talking to your visitors in the future, to entice them back.)*

To achieve all this, the home page needs to combine a good navigational structure with a host of elements that all work together.

Some of the key elements include:

- *Logo*
- *Branding*
- *Opening statement (or value proposition)*
- *Photos of products*
- *Photos of people*
- *'Established since' date*
- *Time, date and personalised message*
- *Landline phone number*
- *Safe shopping symbols*
- *Testimonials*
- *Guarantees*
- *Search box*
- *Buyers guides, videos and other downloads*
- *Polls, lists, competitions and competition winners*
- *FAQs link*
- *Buy Now buttons*
- *Newsletter sign-ups*
- *Request a quote/call back buttons*
- *Ask the expert*
- *Promotions and special offers*
- *Checkout*

How these elements work together

Each of these individual elements has a specific function, which generally falls into one or more of these four broad categories

FUNCTION	Example
Attract attention or create awareness	Value proposition, main photograph
Build trust and reduce risk	Branding, 'Established since' date
Generate interest	Photographs of bestsellers, competitions
Encourage the viewer to take action	Newsletter sign-up, special offers

These classifications are not rigid, and many of the elements cross over to fulfil more than one function. The logo, for example, if it is well-known, can create awareness and also engender a feeling of trust. Promotions help to get your viewer interested in buying as well as encouraging them to buy now. No single element is especially strong by itself, but carefully placed they all work together to support each other and lead the customer to take action, funneling them towards making a purchase.

Placing the elements

So where should they all go for maximum effect? There are endless ways to design a website, but even though the internet is relatively young, certain conventions are starting to become established. Usability studies all over the world have shown that people respond to websites in remarkably similar ways wherever they live. Just as cities in every country tend to have signposts and traffic lights in similar places, so more and more websites are being built that have a similar structure and navigation.

On the next page is a template diagram showing where today's internet shoppers expect to find many of these different elements. Not surprisingly, the most important elements go at the top, because people tend to scan the upper part of the page first. Placing them here helps to establish, at a glance, what the site has to offer and how to find it. A format like this keeps the home page relatively clean and uncluttered, with the main focus on the middle of the page where you want it – on an enticing display of products

Of course, these are only guidelines, not gospel, and you can choose to break the rules. However, several of my clients who have adopted this kind of framework have found it improves their sales.

In the rest of the chapter, we go on to look at these individual elements in more detail.

Template - website home page

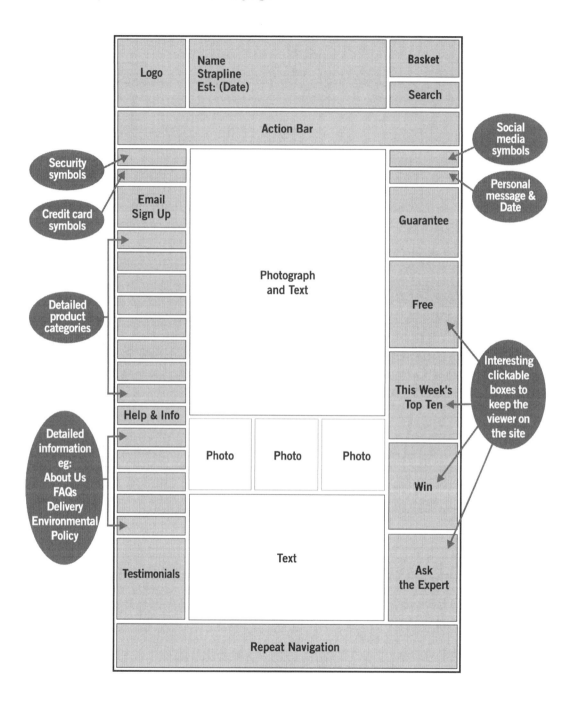

■ A conventional 3-column layout with C-navigation, showing typical placements for key elements.

Elements that attract attention or create awareness

These elements work by letting the visitor know immediately what they will find on the site and why they should stay.

Logo

Your logo brings your brand to life (although, of course, your brand is so much more than just your logo). The conventional place for your logo is the top left hand corner. Nowadays most sites are constructed with the logo on every single page of the site and clicking on it takes the viewer straight back to the home page.

Branding

This is not so much a single element as a collection of factors that together make the website recognisably yours and create a feeling or impression in the mind of your visitor. The logo is part of this, but so too is the overall look, colour palette, fonts and layout, photographic style and tone of voice of the copy.

The best websites let the viewer know at a glance whether the brand is luxury or bargain basement, the sort of products on offer and the ethos and personality of the company. There should be some synergy with your other marketing material, like your catalogue, ads, prospecting leaflets, mailshots and email newsletters so you get the cumulative benefit of repeated viewings by your customer.

Statement

Often known as an 'online value proposition' the statement is a message that tells the visitor quickly and succinctly what the site is for and what it can offer them. It's needed because the casual visitor can't be expected to guess just from photographs. A website showing photos of dogs could be selling pet food or pet-friendly cottages, so a short line can help make it clear fast, eg:

- *Your one-stop shop for top quality pet food*
- *Britain's best selection of dog-friendly cottages*

The statement should be short and clear rather than trying to be clever. Web users want instant information not riddles. According to Tim Ash, author of Landing Page Optimisation, the majority of internet users scan a web page rather than reading it. They are task-oriented and zoom in on individual words or phrases.

Even more important, it should tell the customer precisely what the benefit is for them. What is it that makes your product unique? How does it improve the life of the person using it? How does your product make the world a better place?

Your home page opening statement is like a headline of an ad, summing up the benefits and making you want to read on. The only difference is that an ad headline can grab attention

with wordplay, but on the web you have to get to the point. In the pet food example above, a statement like "Yum yum. Woof woof." might work well as an ad headline, but it's too opaque for a website.

Remember that not everyone coming to your site will know you or what you can do for them. Even your existing customers never tire of hearing why they're making the right choice to buy from you. No matter how brilliant you've been in the past there's always the nagging, unspoken concern that you may not be as good next time so keep on reassuring them that you care and never take their loyalty for granted.

Photos of your bestsellers

Your home page, rather like the front cover of your catalogue, is your shop window display, so best-in-class sites show a selection of their most desirable merchandise.

People love bestsellers – that's why they sell well. So it stands to reason that displaying these star products on your home page makes people more interested in delving into the site than if you show some dust-gathering old stock that no one wants to buy.

Don't be tempted to use your valuable home page to get rid of slow sellers. It's risky, as if they are genuinely unpopular (rather than not promoted properly) it will discourage people from staying on your site.

Some clients worry about this becoming a self-fulfilling prophecy where you simply sell more of the good products with no chance to clear other stock or introduce new products. However, the main thing at this stage is to get people interested, otherwise you have no chance of selling anything. New products will always be important, as existing customers like the excitement of innovation, and it gives them a reason to keep on checking into your site.

Photos of people

If you're looking for a quick and easy way to get your website to perform better then put a photo of a real person on it. This phenomenon – and the psychology behind it – has been repeatedly observed by Amy Africa and her team at Eight by Eight, one of America's leading usability firms. Their subjects are not merely asked what they think of websites, but are given real money and told to make genuine purchases. Whatever they buy they can keep – sometimes cars or even houses are on offer. It's about as close as you can get to replicating a real buying experience in a laboratory setting.

Research shows that when human beings use the internet they feel surprisingly insecure. It all goes back to the primitive part of our brains that takes hold of our responses at a subconscious level. Like the wary caveman walking in a primeval forest, we treat the internet as if it were an unknown territory with danger lurking round every corner.

One way to calm that and relax the subconscious brain is to provide evidence that other people have trodden the same path. Pictures of people achieve this. In fact, showing a friendly face makes your visitors stay longer and is one of the single best things you can do to improve your site.

▦ Adding photos of people to this site helped improve sales.

One company, Bathroomtrade.co.uk, replaced its bright yellow graphics and nondescript pictures of shower trays with photos of a smiling telesales operator and a man in overalls, and never looked back. If this little trick sounds too good to be true, just because it's cheap and easy, then I can only recommend that you try it for yourself – you've got nothing to lose.

Elements that reduce risk and build trust

The function of trust-building elements is to make people feel secure about shopping with you. Trust has always been important in selling. In the middle ages, when most people bought directly from the producer, villagers knew which tradesmen they could rely on and who was watering down their beer or bulking up their flour with chalk.

With distance selling customers need other clues to reassure them of the quality of the products and the reliability of the company delivering it. Whether it's a mailing pack, catalogue or website, all kinds of fears come into the mind of the customer every time they contemplate buying: "Will it arrive? Will it come on time? What if the quality isn't as good as they claim? What if it's damaged, or the wrong size, or I simply don't like it?"

These fears are felt most strongly when buying over the internet. A catalogue is intrinsically trusted because it is something tangible that feels like there are real people behind it. However, a website is impersonal. Anyone can set one up in a flash and simply disappear once they've taken your money.

In addition there is the 'reptilian brain' response that gets hold of human beings when they're surfing the web, making them especially nervous and flighty, especially at the very moment when they're about to make the purchase.

Devices to make potential customers trust you online are far more important than ever before. You simply cannot give people enough reassurance. Branding, of course, plays a big part, as people trust brands. Fifteen years ago, no-one had heard of Amazon, but now the name has come to mean something, and one of those things is absolute certainty that your goods will turn up in good condition.

But carefully nurtured branding is not the only way to invoke trust and reduce risk on your site. Here are some other devices you can use.

Logo and 'Established since…'

As well as creating awareness, a logo can help build trust, especially if it has been seen elsewhere such as in a catalogue. The design itself, if well done, sends out positive signals. Near the logo is also a good place to add the words 'Established since (date)'. The unwritten message is "We've been going for ages, so we'll still be here tomorrow. Other people have trusted us for years and so can you". Not a bad take-out for just three tiny words.

Time, date and personalised message

Displaying the current time and date makes the site look well maintained, like a coat of new paint. A personal message like 'Welcome back, Mel Henson' helps to give the impression of efficient service and people behind the screen who care – and people always read their own name.

Customer service phone number and social links

It's worth displaying your phone number prominently on the site because it suggests a solid, reliable organisation running the website. If your contact details are easy to find, it increases the chances of your customer acting right away rather than forgetting about it – which means you lose the sale.

If you use social media for customer service, then this too should be featured prominently at the top of the home page. Don't worry that this might encourage people to spend their time tweeting rather than buying online. In fact they're more likely to buy because you've made them feel secure. If they do have a query which you solve with a promptly-answered tweet you're more likely to get the sale.

Safe Shopping symbols and Privacy Statements

Sometimes people are put off buying from your site for fear that their credit card details or personal data will be compromised in some way. Padlocks, hacker-secure images and statements about how well protected your site is all help to knock down these barriers to buying. Robust, positive and consumer-friendly statements about how you protect transactions and data all help when it comes to making people feel confident enough to part with their money.

Testimonials

Endorsements by other people have worked well since the dawn of direct marketing, only falling out of favour during the eighties, when ads with pure image and no copy became all the rage.

Testimonials are now starting to come back into fashion, thanks to internet reviews, social media and internet shopping. Consumers have become accustomed to reading reviews of products by other customers either on-site or off-site on blogs, forums and social media like Twitter and Facebook.

Testimonials, these days, are no longer just gushing heaps of praise; because they represent real opinions by real consumers they tend to give the good, the bad and the ugly. (In fact, the plain good is rarely worthy of comment, as people are more likely to write a review when they've been outraged by a terrible experience or bowled over by a brilliant one.) Customers are now suspicious of any testimonial that seems too glowing; they are more likely to trust an honest appraisal.

So where does this leave testimonials in the context of your home page? Despite customers' assertions that they find 'warts and all' descriptions more believable, it's still sensible to pick positive descriptions. On the home page, show a general testimonial about your company or the overall quality of products or service, leaving more specific testimonials for product or checkout pages. Make it short – just a 'soundbite' extract of a few words that can be clicked on to read the full text.

■ This website for designer dogwear **Love My Dog** has short extracts on the home page. Clicking on it leads through to the full testimonial.

Guarantees

Guarantees are hugely underused and can be one of the most powerful ways you can boost sales. It is a promise to your customer about your products and service, expressed in a way that gives them confidence to make the purchase. It should appear on every piece of marketing material you produce; your website, your catalogue, your order forms and so on.

The words need to be clear and convincing with a tone of voice that is in tune with the rest of the brand. Your guarantee should be in the fonts, colour palette and overall feel of your corporate guidelines. Plus, for it to have 'at-a-glance' weight it is helpful if it has some of the graphic devices that give bank notes and certificates their authority such as seals, ribbons, watermarks and signatures. For some examples, see Chapter 4 (page 63).

A guarantee is simply drawing attention to positive aspects of your customer service that you're probably offering as a matter of course. If someone changes their mind about one of your products, chances are you're more than happy to exchange it or give a refund. If they have a problem, you'd go to great lengths to put it right. A guarantee is a great way to reassure your customers and prospective buyers that you have their best interests at heart.

Social media and blog links

Social media links – Twitter, Facebook, and Digg logos for example – are fast becoming the norm, as though a site without them is in some way a little bit suspect. Conversely their presence sends out the subliminal message that the site is well maintained by real people. It's all these little details that add up to making your visitor feel comfortable about staying on the site.

Perpetual basket

A perpetual (or persistent) basket is simply one that stays on the site, in the same place, whichever page your visitor is on. It shows the number of items in the basket and a running total of the cost. From the moment a product is added to the basket there should be a perpetual 'checkout now' button too. It needs an icon that denotes 'secure shopping' and links to 'view basket', 'print basket contents' and 'save basket' so that the shopper can come back later if they wish.

Ideally there should be two of these perpetual baskets, one at the top right hand corner and an identical one at the bottom right hand corner, so that one or other of them can be seen even when the viewer has scrolled down. Some sites even have three.

Another reason for making sure you can 'save the basket' is so that if your visitor leaves without buying you can send an email later to encourage them to complete the transaction. There are many reasons why people abandon their basket. Sometimes they simply don't realise they hadn't pressed the button to buy, or they might press the 'close' rather than the 'back' button by mistake. Others get interrupted mid-purchase by the phone ringing or something on the stove boiling over. Often they get up to fetch their wallet from another room, get distracted on the way and it slips their mind. So it's worth following these up, as it's money sitting on the table that's relatively inexpensive to recover.

One leading UK fashion firm gets a 27% response rate to their 'abandoned basket' follow up emails, according to Dan Croxen-John of specialist home shopping analytics agency AWA. However he cautions that this approach only works if the email takes the customer back to the original basket, so you have to be able to store the details.

Incidentally, I call it a 'basket', because that's the word we Brits seem to prefer. The Americans call it a 'cart' and the British equivalent would be 'trolley', but that's not a term that's caught on. However, I do like the Marshalls website, a leading supplier of plants, which says 'Add to wheelbarrow'.

Elements that generate interest

Having grabbed the attention of your visitor, you now need to keep him or her interested. These are some of the elements that help to turn a casual viewer into a potential shopper

Their function is to keep visitors wanting to stay on your site and funnel them towards taking an action such as leaving their email address, drilling down to the next level, and ultimately placing an order.

Merchandise

Usability research by Amy Africa of Eight by Eight shows that the ideal number of products to feature on your home page is around eight to ten. Of these, about three to five should be bestsellers because they're great for getting your site noticed and getting people interested. Mixed in with these can be new products, exclusive items, sale bargains and possibly products with an interesting story.

Backwards navigation

These are devices to help your user know where they are in the site and hop around more easily. The simplest is 'breadcrumbs', the little trail of words at the top of the page.

Breadcrumbs: On this example from **Donald Russell**, the breadcrumb trail shows that the user drilled down from the Home page to Lamb and Mutton, then to New Lamb products and finally Lamb Racks.

Recently viewed items also help with navigation and keep people interested. Your visitors are much more likely to buy something they've already seen, so if you can find a way to keep that product in view, it helps smooth the way to the sale.

Efficient search

Although some people always use the search facility on a website, most people tend to use it as a fall-back when the navigation isn't clear or when they're in a real hurry.

There are two kinds of search: 'Search By' (or 'Shop By') filters that allow people to look for the items grouped according to selected criteria, and an open-ended 'Search Box' where they can type in anything and see what comes up.

Search By On a website selling wine, this function might allow the visitor to search by colour (red, white, rosé etc), country (France, Australia, Chile etc), region (Bordeaux, Burgundy etc), grape variety, Chateau/producer, vintage, size (eg: only showing half bottles or magnums), price and so on. The filters can also be set up to allow searches for particular combinations, such as red wine from Australia in half bottles costing under £10.

Search Box. The other type of search allows people to key in any word, phrase or catalogue number. This is great when it works, but on some sites the on-site search fails up to half the time, leading to frustrated, disillusioned visitors who you'll never turn into customers.

Making your on-site search efficient and user-friendly is a combination of design, technology and copy. Good design helps by putting the search box in an easy-to-find place and using graphics like a magnifying glass for instant recognition. (Icons help a lot because people are more likely to notice pictures on websites rather than text).

If you have an excellent search facility which returns meaningful results for your customers virtually every time, then the search box can be placed smack bang in the middle column at the top. (This is where Amazon usually puts it). However, if you know your search has some flaws, then it's better positioned at the top of the left hand column under the email sign-up box.

Failed search alternatives

Technology is improving all the time with clever schemes to reduce the number of failed searches. These are the times when the system comes back with 'no results found' or something irrelevant such as diamond rings when someone types in 'curtain rings'. For those times when a customer mis-spells or uses vague descriptions, the site can include a dictionary to give "Did you mean..." prompts, and a thesaurus to suggest alternative terms.

It's always better to show the customer something on their 'no finds' even if it's just a suggestion to browse the A-Z product list. An effective policy is to suggest generic recommendations for alternative products or show the top ten bestsellers. According to analytics expert Dan Croxen-John of Applied Web Analytics, this works significantly better if they are genuine best-sellers based on analysis of your own data, rather than just picking items at random.

Search messages

When a search doesn't come up with what the customer wants you can use copy to create a better on-site search experience. A blunt message like "No results found..." can make your visitor feel criticised, as though they have failed in some way. Irrational as it sounds, they blame you or resent you for it and feel let down by your brand.

Softer words like "We didn't find..." imply that you did your best to help and above all that it's not your visitor's fault. Show you care by starting a phrase with "Sorry..." (or "Doh!.." or "Ooops..." if those are appropriate to the brand personality).

Try to avoid using the word 'results' which sounds impersonal and technical and instead repeat back their own search term. Instead of, "Sorry, no results found" try going for "Sorry, we didn't find any curtain rings". It's a helpful reminder of what the customer was searching for and helps them feel comfortable and in control.

You can go one step further with a live-chat for failed searches or a call-back button "Click here and one of us will phone you to help you find what you need". If you have their email address you can send an email along the lines of, "Sorry we couldn't find any curtain rings. Could you let us know what sort of curtain rings you were looking for as we may be able to help?"

Just as important is to reward your visitor when they have successful searches, with phrases like, "Good news: You have 26 curtain rings to choose from". It may sound a little patronising but it works because it soothes and flatters the sub-conscious part of the user's brain that research shows is relied on so much when shopping on the internet.

Analysis shows these little touches encourage your visitors to spend longer on a site so the sooner they're in place, the sooner they can start helping to contribute to the bottom line.

Free downloads and buyers guides

Increasingly there's a school of thought that the best way to sell through the internet is by giving things away. By that I don't mean lots of free gifts or 'Buy one get one free' but rather information which is genuinely useful to your potential customer. Typically, it is in the form of a web page, a pdf or a sound or video recording.

On a website these can be offered as either a 'lead-capture' download or a 'click-thru'. Downloads give you the chance to capture the user's email address so you can contact that person again in the future. The click-thru doesn't as it's simply a link or button that takes the viewer straight through to the document.

Although click-thrus don't let you build up your mailing list, they increase the chances of getting the message read as they're quicker and easier for the customer to access than a download. They also have the benefit of helping your natural search engine optimisation, by adding to the mass of 'high quality content' on your site that helps you get higher rankings.

Buyer's guides are excellent to help you become firmly rooted in the mind of the customer as a trusted place to buy. Another benefit is that they can help to reduce the amount of time your customer services team spend on the phone by providing the answers to questions that often come up.

They are particularly good where the customer is likely to spend some time doing research, for items such as furniture, bathroom fittings and garden equipment. Detailed, impartial information is just what people are looking for when they're starting to think about buying a new sofa, wetroom or summer house. When they're ready to buy, your site is more likely to be on the shortlist because they know and trust you.

Increasingly buyer's guides are being produced as videos rather than the written word. Google gives higher rankings to sites with video, and they're brilliant in communities, forums and all social media.

■ Donald Russell's Head Chef explains on video how to cook the perfect steak.

Donald Russell, the leading online butcher, regularly uses video for topics such as 'How to cook a turkey' and 'How to cook the perfect steak'. According to director Ian Morrison the key to success is "Make them short and make them relevant. Use your communities and forums to find out what people really want to know."

Frequently Asked Questions

FAQs are one of the most viewed parts of any site, and often one of the first pages to be clicked on by new visitors. The questions should be worded and laid out in such a way as to immediately give the casual visitor an overview of what you do and why they should buy from you. You can also use this section to weave in more requests for the visitor to give you their email address.

Take as much time over planning and designing your FAQs page as any of the other pages, and it will repay your efforts in spades. For more ideas on how to craft your FAQs see chapter 7 (page 108).

Delivery charges and return policies

Every month, untold millions of sales are lost by people changing their minds about buying when they have to hunt around for the delivery charges. The easier you can make it for people to find this information the better. If your charges are high, it causes bad feeling to keep this fact hidden until the last stage of the checkout process. If your charges are low, or free, tell the world. You'll get more sales. Even if your delivery is only free above a certain spend, it's fine to headline with copy such as "FREE DELIVERY – when you spend £X".

Elements that encourage action

The most beautiful website in the world is useless if it doesn't get your visitors doing something. Of course the ultimate action is to make a purchase but that's not always the first objective. Websites work as a funnel, gradually moving visitors closer and closer towards a sale. With analytics programmes, there is enormous scope for measuring practically every keystroke and click of the user, each one a series of small steps towards the main goal.

Each of these micro-actions or conversions is measurable and each has a clear value. It could be how often visitors click through to a particular page, download a buyer's guide, watch a video, or sign up for a newsletter. It can even be as simple as spending a certain amount of time on specific pages or filling in a form.

Here are some of the elements that are specifically concerned with nudging people to take action.

Action buttons

These include 'Buy Now', 'Add to Basket', and 'More Details'. Take care with the copy on these buttons to make sure the instructions are absolutely clear. If the button doesn't let your customer buy immediately, don't label it 'Buy Now' but 'Add to Basket' or 'More Info' or whatever is an accurate reflection of what really happens when they click the button.

Action buttons should be as big as you can possibly bear without ruining the design. According to research by Amy Africa, red is the action colour proven to get more clicks than other colours, especially yellow, the colour of fear, which should be avoided.

Make sure you have some 'Buy Now' or 'Add to Basket' buttons on show when your visitor lands. Since only 30% of people scroll down, it needs to be visible in the first screen view (known rather quaintly as 'above the fold' as though the web page is a sort of broadsheet newspaper). In all of these action buttons, the word 'NOW' is very powerful, because it's an embedded command which encourages the brain to take action, so 'Buy Now' is always better than 'Submit Order'.

Free downloads

If you've gone to the trouble of putting together an information document, then go hell for leather to get people to download it. Pop it in the right hand column, give it a snappy title, and display it prominently with bright, well designed graphics.

Certain titles are perennially popular, such as:

- *How to . . .*
- *Your guide to . . .*
- *Choosing . . . made easy*

Numbers are also good, such as

- *5 easy ways to . . .*
- *7 secrets of . . .*
- *8 things to watch out for before you buy a . . .*
- *9 facts about . . .*
- *The top 10 . . .*
- *21 tips and tricks of . . .*

Anyone who is seriously in the market for one of your products will want to get hold of downloads like these that promise quick, easy-to-read and valuable information.

Newsletter sign-ups

It's a real bonus if you can get someone to sign up for your newsletter. They are effectively saying "Yes please, get in touch with me. I want to hear from you." and will be your best source of future business. Make your newsletter sign-up as attractive as possible to get as many names as you can, and make the box appear on every page (until they have signed up – then it should disappear). Newsletter sign-ups, free downloads and other lead-capturing devices should be present in all four quarters of the page.

Perpetual basket

We looked at the perpetual (or persistent) basket earlier when dissecting what elements make a website trustworthy. It is repeated again here, because it has a secondary function in creating interest and desire by signalling very clearly "Here are things for sale", and "We want you to buy". It changes the mindset of the visitor without them even realising it and encourages them to take action.

Right hand column

Not all websites have a right hand column, as it's only possible when you have a three-column layout, with one wide column in the middle and two narrow ones either side. Eye-tracking studies show that there is a natural tendency for web users to focus in the middle of a site so this format directs attention to where you want it – on your products.

Three column layouts may not be to everyone's taste, but more 'beautiful' designs using the whole width of the page leave your visitor with only one or two places to look at. They can quickly decide they've seen everything and leave. Three columns have more to help keep their interest. If you're not sure, it's easy to test one design against another.

This structure also allows you to use the right hand side as a 'saviour column' to save people from leaving. As mentioned before when discussing navigational structure, the left hand column and top and bottom rows (the 'C' of your 'C-navigation') should remain constant, but your right hand column needs to change often to keep it fresh.

On some sites, the right hand column looks like a series of mini ads or posters, with a headline and benefit statement. Each one should have a clickable action button at the bottom of the box to encourage people to drill deeper so that they stay on the site.

Things that tend to do well are:

- *Teasers*
- *Facts*
- *Quizzes*
- *Polls*
- *Competitions and previous winners*
- *'Ask the Experts'*
- *Games and point-collecting devices*
- *Lists, such as the top 5 best sellers or recently viewed items*
- *Special limited time offer*
- *Free e-books*

Devices like these give the impression that the site is well-used, which in turn makes it look more trustworthy. Polls can be as simple as 'Do you prefer fried eggs broken-yolk or sunny side up?' or more serious, 'Did we give you service with a smile?'. Lists might be your customers' top ten all time favourite products, last week's best sellers or top five new products.

Featuring the lucky winners from a competition that was previously featured on the website is a great way to make the site look well tended. If possible, show photos or even videos of their happy faces as they claim their prize.

Easy to use checkout

When I was cutting my teeth in direct marketing at Ogilvy & Mather Direct, we went to endless lengths to make coupons in press ads or mailing packs as easy as possible to fill in. More time went into designing it than any other part of the creative work with the express aim of making it look as quick and easy as possible. Anything complicated was ruthlessly weeded out. The customer didn't want to spend hours filling in a long form, they wanted to get it over and done with as quickly as possible.

Human reactions to a website checkout process are just the same. The quicker and easier it looks the more people will buy, which is one reason why nowadays very few websites insist on a customer having to register before they can buy.

One of the differences between a checkout process and a pen and ink coupon is that the customer knows exactly how long the offline version will take to fill in. With the online equivalent, they don't. It's therefore vital to give back this control by explaining what stage the customer is at and how much longer there is to go.

To make the checkout faster, use pre-filled information as much as possible, and design the form with vertical capture fields. It's easier to fill out an online form when you're just going in one direction (down) rather than left to right and down.

Landing pages

The home page is not always the page your visitor arrives at or 'lands on' when they first come to your site. In fact, they can arrive on almost any page. To continue the store analogy, it's a bit like a large department store with one grand front entrance and lots of smaller doors on the side streets.

Bricks and mortar stores try to give all these side entrances a welcoming feel and distinctive look. In the same way, every page of the site needs to maintain some of the key elements of the home page, including design features, navigation, perpetual basket and security features. It makes people feel comfortable and secure, which means they stay longer.

Specially designed landing pages

If your landing page has been specially created to tie in with an ad or an email campaign then it's important for the customer journey that the landing page recognises where they've come from. If you've sent an email showing a picture of a boot, make sure it clicks through to the same boot. Don't dump your customer in the middle of a general website with the promised special offer nowhere in sight.

For your customer, that's a bit like being handed a leaflet in the street with the promise of a special offer at a particular store, then getting to the shop and finding all the shop assistants looking blank and shaking their heads. The customer feels deflated or conned and certainly wouldn't want to visit the store again. If instead they're greeted with someone saying, "Hello. I see you've got one of our leaflets. Just hand it to the cashier when you pay to get your discount", they'll feel welcome, confident and in the mood for shopping.

Your landing page is exactly the same. All it needs is a simple greeting that recognises what brought the customer in such as "Thank you for clicking through from the email we sent you" or "Welcome – this is the Daily Telegraph special offer". The products featured should match the products in the promotion. This instantly tells the reader they are in the right place, which makes them feel safe, appreciated and in control which in turn helps them look forward to buying. Research shows that this has a real effect on sales. In tests, bounce rates have been shown to drop a massive 25% just by changing the landing page.

Product pages

When someone has clicked through to a particular product page, they are in a very different mindset from when they first landed or are just clicking around. Rather like a butterfly coming into your garden, they begin by flitting here and there, and eventually alight on a tasty flower to drink the nectar. The likelihood is that they are now seriously interested in your product and prepared to give it some proper attention.

Most of the time people don't read in depth on the web, they scan. This is the moment where they stop skimming and start to dive in. If your customer were in a shop, this is equivalent to when they pick up something from the shelf. The job now is to convince them that this product is just right for them, and they can trust you to sell it to them. They are hungry for information such as:

- *What the product looks like, which comes down to photography that shows the product clearly from a number of angles. This is functional photography. It can be artistic, beautifully lit and styled, but must give the customer a proper idea of what it looks like. Technologies like zoom and video are great for this.*

- *The main benefit of this particular product. How will it improve their life?*

- *The main benefit of buying it from you rather than anyone else.*

- *Sensory details that are not immediately obvious from the photo (but would be obvious if they were able to feel and touch it in a store) such as the softness, the weight, the warmth, the taste.*

- *Practical details, including sizes, colours, specification.*

- *Availability and stock levels.*

- *Delivery information, including cost, speed and returns policy.*

They will also be extremely interested in (and influenced by):

- *Testimonials and customer reviews.*

- *Case studies and survey results (if appropriate).*

- *Complementary products*
  ("You might also like…", "Our designer suggests…", "Customers who bought this also bought…" and so on. Incidentally, several of my clients have found that when these are based on genuine customer data, they do many times better than if you just guess at it or pick products at random).

- *After-sales service and guarantees (if appropriate).*

And of course, for your own benefit, you will want to ask for the order on every single product page, with lots of 'Buy Now' and 'Add to Basket' buttons.

If this seems like a lot to get on to a single product page, then remember that it doesn't need to be dense blocks of text. One of the great things about the web is the possibility for different messages to be made larger or smaller simply by scrolling over them with a mouse

The customer can look at one big image, and scroll over thumbnails of other angles to make them the main image instead. They can also zoom in or enlarge the photo.

Even large chunks of text can be made easy to scan by using bullet points, sub-heads and quick facts. Testimonials and delivery information don't need to be in the centre of the screen, they can go in the columns at the sides.

Tabbed notes let the user jump from one type of information to another without leaving the page, or even the view. Used by many sites, including designer clothes website, Net-a-Porter, these 'pages-within-a-page' have clickable tabs with headings like 'Buyer's notes', 'Detailed spec', 'Size and weight' and 'Care instructions'.

Social spaces, social media, blogs and forums

With more than three quarters of all companies using social media, most self-respecting websites now have some kind of social media presence as well as their own blogs and communities.

A quarter of all time spent on the internet is now devoted to social media. However, the way social media is used, especially by businesses, and how it inter-relates with the main website is changing all the time. It's a certainty that by the time you read this it will be out of date. However, with the expert help of Charlie Osmond of Fresh Networks, here is some of the best advice on social media right now.

What is social media?

Social media encompasses websites and webspaces that allow people to connect with each other. Much of the content is created and driven by users, by pages they create, words they write and links they forward to each other (rather than by the site owner).

Some of the biggest and most well known social sites are Facebook, Myspace, Youtube, Twitter and Friends Reunited. Customer reviews on Amazon and iTunes also form part of the social media world. However, the key to understanding social media is realising that it's not about the technology, it's about human beings and how they interact.

From an e-commerce point of view there are a variety of different types of people who use social media. These are some of the ways you can segment your audience.

- *Fans*
- *Influencers*
- *Advocates who want help*
- *Enemies who want to damage your brand*
- *Current customers (both satisfied and dissatisfied)*
- *Potential customers looking for your product*

The way to cater for all segments or people is a combination of pro-actively managing your own social space (a forum, blog or community), integrating your social media with your website and email campaigns, and being vigilant about monitoring other social media and responding appropriately.

Networks and Communities

At one time, it looked as if social media could be divided between business and private, with sites like LinkedIn for business and Facebook for leisure. However, now that many organisations have their own Facebook pages it's not always useful to view it in this way.

Perhaps a more useful distinction is the difference between networks and communities. Social networks tend to be focussed on 'me and my connections to other people'. The members take actions, view content or make comments because of who they are connected to and what those people have done. This includes the social networking sites Facebook and MySpace as well as business networking sites such as LinkedIn. Here, the relationships with other people within the network are important.

Online Communities are about 'Us'. People come together around a common goal or share common interests, but aren't really interested in who the other people are. These include review communities on Amazon and Trip Advisor and specialist interest sites such as the Royal Horticultural Society. If you want to chat or get advice about flowers, you don't mind if a complete stranger chimes in as long as they're of like mind. Increasingly, these can also be company forums, such as ASOS Life, where anyone can chat about ASOS products or fashion in general.

Social media and sales

Of course, as a business, you're naturally interested in how you can harness social media to boost the bottom line. At the moment, measuring any sort of return on investment is proving difficult and few firms achieve a direct return on social media. Even the big boys haven't yet cracked this particular nut. Disney's Toy Story 3 ran an expensive and very high profile social media campaign which was brilliant at generating 'online buzz' but didn't translate through to box office sales.

Fans of social media argue that looking for profits from social media is missing the point and that the greatest returns will come from long-term relationship building, not quick-win viral videos. Chasing short-term Return on Investment (ROI) leads to insincere behaviour in the social web which can actually turn people off your brand. So what can social media do for your business?

Functions of social media

Social media can be useful in many different roles including:

- ◆ *Customer service*
- ◆ *Driving sales and leads*
- ◆ *Natural search*
- ◆ *Insight (ethnographic market research)*
- ◆ *Innovation (ideas for service, new products or new uses for old products)*
- ◆ *Advocacy (awareness, brand building, PR, engagement, internal morale)*

Of these, perhaps the most valuable (and most likely to give you potential cost savings) is customer service. Social media is a bit like a telephone in the sense that it is a tool to connect people for a conversation. The difference is that anyone can join in, everyone can see everything that's been said and they can search for the bits of conversation that interest them.

Social media for customer service

Using Twitter or your own forums to answer customer queries is a bit like everyone in the world being able to listen in to your call-centre – and choose the calls they listen to. The worry is that customers can see everything that's being said about you – good and bad. But that's part of the new rules of engagement, a fact of life in today's digital world. The reality is that it doesn't matter so much if negative things are said about you – in fact, it helps build up trust because you're seen as 'real'. What's important is how you're seen to deal with those complaints.

That's why social media plays such a key role in customer service. Imagine that one of your customers posts a tweet (either on Twitter or your own forum – it shouldn't matter as they should all be linked so that whatever is input into one also shows on the other). If this is a complaint, other people may have exactly the same problem, so they can find out straight away what to do about it.

The fact that social media is so instant makes it especially useful in a crisis. Airports are already finding Twitter invaluable to give immediate information when flights are disrupted. Each time you make a sale, why not suggest that the customer follows you on Twitter? Encourage them to ask for updates to their phone. It opens up a cost-effective, quick way to let customers know about any hiccups, either one-to-one about individual orders or globally such as when a courier strike threatens to delay many orders.

Even more importantly it builds huge trust and credibility for your brand, simply because you are seen to be dealing with the problem. It's long been known that customers who have a bad experience which is handled well go on to become your most loyal fans, and tell lots of people. Evidence suggests that the same goes for potential customers. Even though they didn't have the experience themselves, simply witnessing it can help turn them into loyal customers who spend more and buy more frequently.

Summary

Your home page needs to quickly establish your brand and what you have to offer. It should also include elements to grab the attention of your visitor, win their trust, coax their interest in you and encourage them to take some actions.

Your navigation accounts for up to 60% of the success of your site, so it's vital to get it right.

Conventional C-navigation has been shown to be extremely effective and easy to use.

Always show a perpetual basket – two or three times if possible.

Ask for the email address lots of times, in lots of different ways. It's crucial to help build up your database of customers for the future.

Use the right hand column to entice your visitors to stay just as they're about to leave the site.

Using the internet can cause anxiety because the subconscious part of our brains sees it as unfamiliar territory. People buy more when they're relaxed, so it's important to make your visitors feel safe and secure. One way to do this is to show evidence that other people have been to your site and done the same as them, such as photographs, reviews and testimonials.

Social media is becoming the norm on websites and has a wide range of roles to play. It is especially useful for customer service. Communities, networks and blogs all have different functions, but they all help with long term relationship branding rather than instant and measurable return on investment.

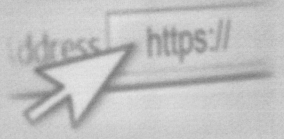

1 | **Anatomy of a website**

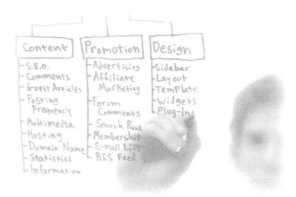

2 | How to plan your web pages

Planning the structure and navigation of your web pages is a bit like building a house. Unlike every other medium including catalogues, press, TV and radio, websites are a 3-D space. Your site is like a virtual building with pages for rooms, and the links to act as lifts, stairs and secret passageways going from one room to another. The challenge is to show this 3-D structure on a two-dimensional piece of paper.

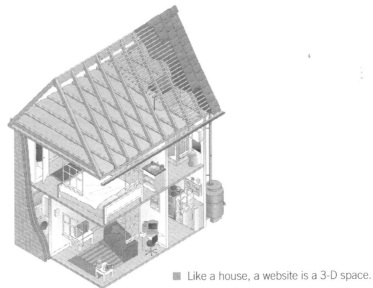

■ Like a house, a website is a 3-D space.

A building always has some parts that have to be in a particular place, such as an entrance door on the ground floor. These are the equivalent of the static pages and checkout. Then there are many other elements that can go almost anywhere and in any arrangement such as rooms and corridors. These are the equivalent of your category pages and product pages.

It makes sense, therefore to start the planning by looking at which static pages are to be included and where they might go, such as:

- *Home page*
- *About us*
- *Contact us*
- *Special offers*
- *News*
- *Environmental policy, Privacy and so on*

The more complex part of the planning is to decide where the products will go. Rather like planning a catalogue, there are four key steps.

The four-step process of planning web pages

1. **Listing:** *List all your products.*
2. **Grouping:** *Group into categories.*
3. **Naming and Linking:** *Finalise names and decide internal links from one product to another.*
4. **Allocating:** *Place the static pages, categories, sub-categories and products onto a wire frame, site map or navigation layout.*

Step 1 - Listing

The starting point is to compile a complete list of products to sort into categories. In most companies, lists exist but possibly not in a format that can be easily accessed. Sometimes different pieces of information are held in separate files.

At this stage of the planning, your list needs only single product lines, not all the variants. If you sell toys your list might include yo-yos. You would need each different type of yo-yo, but not necessarily every colour or size each model comes in.

Step 2 - Grouping

The next stage is to group your products according to how people buy. Aim to have as few categories as possible in each level while still being logical from a customer's point of view. American website expert Amy Africa recommends a maximum of around 22-25 categories for your top level.

Sometimes the groupings will be very obvious. A clothing site might have Menswear, Womenswear and Childrenswear. However, it's not always as clear cut as this example. Sometimes you could classify products in one of several ways. Should a wind-up torch go in 'Torches' or 'Eco-Friendly Gadgets' or 'Lighting'? Would you put soap dispensers and soap refills into 'Equipment' and 'Consumables', or put them both into one category called something like 'Health & Hygiene' or 'Bathroom Essentials'?

There are no right or wrong ways to sort your categories, and if you look at your competitors' websites, you'll probably find that each one has structured their categories and classified the products in a different way. (That doesn't mean they're right, or that you should copy them!) The guiding principle is always to know your customers. Try to get into their heads to understand where they might look for things they want to buy.

Keyword research

Usually associated with Adword campaigns or search engine optimised copy, keyword research can also help define the structure of your site, because it helps you understand where customers expect to find things. Using the free Google Adword tool or one of the more sophisticated paid-for tools like WordTracker, you can key in the name of your products and see what other similar items come up. It also gives you clues about what names to give your categories.

Card-sorting

A quick and easy way to organise and plan your categories is to use the card-sorting method. This technique has been successfully used by information architects for over a decade. It can be done on-screen using card-sorting software or manually using good old-fashioned index cards, pens and sticky labels (which, if you've read my introduction, you'll know is a route that holds a lot of appeal for me!)

Write the name of each product on a card, and simply arrange them in piles, putting the cards into groups that seem to belong together. Then give a name to each group. The process can be repeated by other people, such as your customer services team, which often throws up some thought-provoking angles.

One of the reasons why this works so well is that it's the closest you can get to replicating the 3-D element of the finished website. It's quick and easy to shuffle and juggle your products until you get it right. It's also a good way to get categories and sub- categories that are of roughly equal size. A huge pile of cards – or a thin one – is easy to spot, and you can then re-sort to have more equal categories.

Use the same process to sort your main categories into sub-categories. Each sub-category represents a drill-down in the real website – a bit like adding extra floors to the building.

Step 3 –Naming and Linking

When you have all your piles sorted, the categories need to be named. Keyword research can also help you select the most 'findable' terms possible. For example, people tend to key in the word 'gift' rather than 'present' by a factor of around ten to one, so it's preferable to use names like 'Gifts for Men' rather than 'Presents for Men'.

You can also use the cards to work out the internal links that can help improve your search engine rankings for free. Say you decide to put soap dispensers into a 'Bathroom

Equipment' category and soap into a 'Refills' category, then it might be helpful to link them internally (one of the secret passages from one room to another). Simply write on the card where the link will appear and the name of the page it links to (possibly in another colour).

Step 4 – Allocating

Once all the cards are sorted into their categories then the product information can be input into a wireframe or sitemap. There are a number of different software programmes to do this, but it's still common for this to be mapped out on Excel with columns for the static pages, main categories, sub-categories and products, together with the page title and URL.

It's a good idea at this stage to get input from everyone on the team. Chances are that someone will spot a better place for one or two products, simply because there are so many ways to organise your categories. They might also pick up on products that are wrongly classified because of an oversight. Just like building a house, it's much easier to change things now rather than when construction starts.

Planning your home page

Once the categories are agreed and the navigation planned out, work can start on the home page.

First of all take a moment to think about who might land on it. Unlike most creative planning, where you would think in terms of demographics and psychographics, it's more useful at this stage to think of your visitors in terms of their reasons for visiting. Where are they in their buying cycle? The type of visitors that will be coming to your site could include:

- ◆ *Loyal repeat customers* *sitting at the screen, catalogue in hand with all the product codes written down ready to key into your 'Quick Shop' box.*

- ◆ *Existing customers* *who might simply fancy taking a peep at what's new or have something very specific in mind to buy now. Whatever stage of the buying cycle they are at, they want to find what they're looking for quickly and easily.*

- ◆ *Prospective customers* *who may have some knowledge about you, or none at all, depending on how they came across your site. They may be at any stage of the buying cycle. If they're right at the beginning they may be more interested in researching general information. Later on they want to compare products and get details. If they're close to a decision, they'll be looking to find a specific product quickly.*

- ◆ *Shoppers* *wanting to find or visit one of your bricks and mortar retail outlets (if you have them). They simply want the address, phone number and opening hours as quickly as possible.*

- ◆ ***Competitors*** *sniffing around to find out what you're up to.*

- ◆ ***Journalists*** *both friendly and hostile.*

- ◆ ***Job hunters***.

- ◆ ***Employees*** *both past and present.*

- ◆ ***Shareholders***.

- ◆ ***Members of the community***.

It's counter-productive to try and design a good homepage for every one of these types of visitors. You don't need to cater to them all equally. Job hunters are much more motivated to hunt out the careers page, so they will definitely find even the smallest tab somewhere 'below the fold' or any other 'cold' area of the home page. Journalists, employees and shareholders will also seek out what they need.

Even your loyal repeat customers don't need too big a share of the page – they just need to be sure they're in the right place and can find the 'Quick Shop' box easily. Trying to appeal to all the people mentioned above will simply give you a cluttered site where it's hard for any visitor to know what to do. Try to resist the temptation to put too much onto the home page. If you have lots of things all shouting for attention, the effect is a clamour where nothing gets heard. Keep it simple so that the important things are easy to find.

Try to plan your home page for your prime group. If the group you most need to target is prospects then being single-minded about that will allow you to give more weight to capturing their email address (for example, by signing up to a newsletter or downloading a free report).

As long as it doesn't alienate or confuse any of your other types of visitor this single-minded focus will be more effective than one that tries to be all things to all visitors. You can also take some of the pressure off the home page by creating separate landing pages for your Pay Per Click (PPC) traffic, or traffic generated from PR, referrals, affiliate sites, offline advertising and so on. That allows you to have a less cluttered, more streamlined home page, more focussed landing pages and keep more people happy.

Planning your social media integration

There's as much planning needed for a successful social media strategy as any other type of marketing. It can also soak up a big chunk of management and creative time. Social media is not cheap or free; like a well-run website, it is highly resource-intensive.

Firstly, consider why you are investing in social media. Is it to generate leads, capture names or is it to build awareness of your brand? Is it a research tool to help develop new products or improve your service? Do you want to educate your audience? Do you want to reduce customer service calls? Or possibly simply improve morale within the company.

Like any other part of the business, it's worth considering your Key Performance Indicators (KPIs). On social media, these are things like speed of response to customer service queries or comments posted on Twitter and the number of Twitter followers who then go on to your blog.

Social media strategy

A hub and spoke approach is emerging as best practice for some organisations, although it's not the only strategy. At the centre is your managed community hub linked to external communities and networks which are monitored and responded to. Content from the central community can be posted to external sites, and vice versa – provided, of course, it's useful. interesting and admired by your readers.

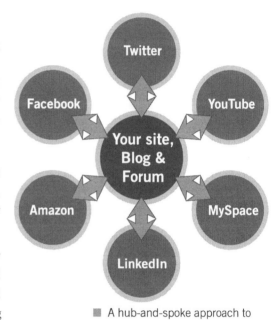

A hub-and-spoke approach to social media on your website.

It's worth considering who within your organisation will 'listen' to all the social media chat and monitor what's being said about your brand. How should that listening be communicated to the team, and even more importantly, how will it then be used in your social media activity?

Content needs to be constantly generated for social media, and it's expected that a lot will come from in-house personnel. How do you plan to motivate your staff to produce content that's engaging and admired by the viewers? There are also some copyright and HR issues around the ownership of these cyber-messages and the persona of the writer.

Some of the other planning considerations include developing a strategy for promotions on social media. How does it tie in with your mainstream marketing? How should offers be presented in a way that is acceptable to social media users, who are notoriously quick to take offence at the slightest sniff of commercial exploitation?

Measuring results

What you decide to measure will depend on your objectives. It's useful to consider from the start how your social media campaign will be measured and how it will be used to improve future activity.

Right now, it's unlikely that these measurements will include sales. So far, I've not come across a company that has managed to correlate the effort and investment in social media with increased sales. It's a holy grail that many are chasing but no-one seems to have worked out the secret – yet!

Summary

Set out your objectives for the site and define your target audience.

There are four stages to planning a web structure. Listing, Grouping, Naming and Allocating

Start with a full list of products. Sort them into groups, according to how people look for products.

Cards can be a good way to sort your categories and decide internal links.

Use keyword research to give names to your categories, pages and URLs.

Be realistic about the business benefits of social media, and be aware of the time and effort needed to keep it maintained.

2 | **How to plan your web pages**

Clicks

3 | **Anatomy of a catalogue**

Now it's time to turn the scalpel on to catalogues and start dissecting them into their individual parts. Your catalogue, even more than your website, is a store without walls. American mail order experts even refer to the top-selling pages as 'prime real estate'. Understanding how it all works together can make the difference between a catalogue that pulls in the sales and one that pulls you under.

Earlier, we looked at the key parts of a website. There are some interesting parallels with the key parts of a catalogue.

This part of a website...	is equivalent to this part of a catalogue
Home Page	Front cover, back cover and spine (or envelope if used) *
Product Pages	Catalogue pages and double page spreads
Static Pages	Inside front cover spread
Checkout	Order form
Landing pages	Mini-catalogues or prospect mailers
Navigation	Overall layout

*Most catalogues are now mailed in a clear polythene envelope or 'naked' with no outer covering, so often the covers are seen first.

We also looked at how elements within the website perform different functions:

- *Attract attention or create awareness*
- *Build trust and reduce risk*
- *Generate interest*
- *Encourage action*

Catalogues also have specific elements designed to influence customers in these ways and move them towards getting their credit card out of their purse. On a website, a lot of the elements can be seen on the homepage. This is essential because of the hierarchical nature of a website – home →category →product →checkout – and the fact that it has to be viewed one page at a time.

A catalogue is multi-layered and can be quickly viewed in its entirety, so the elements tend to be more evenly spread out. Each individual part of the catalogue displays some of the elements that perform these functions, but so too does the catalogue as a whole. For example, the cover is designed to attract attention, but so too is every spread within.

"Come inside and we will show you more magical things"

Front Cover

Like your landing page or a bricks and mortar store, a cover is your shop window, and should be mouth-wateringly appealing. It has one function: to make the reader rip off the outer plastic covering, turn the page and look inside. Like a website, you have only moments to do this, so it must hint at what you sell and give the reader a promise "Come inside and we will show you more magical things".

There are many ways of doing this – and some of the best covers don't show any of the merchandise on sale inside. The spectrum ranges from hard sell on specific products through to artfully styled products with no price information or even an unrelated image that simply sets a mood. There are no hard and fast rules - all types of cover can be effective, depending on factors like the target audience, time of year and brand positioning.

Hard-working covers that sell off the front page certainly make the most of every square inch of selling space. However, real-life case studies show that covers with an aspirational image or a close-up of a smiling face can perform equally well, if not better. The recent Verdict Consulting research commissioned by Pindar shows that 'magazine' style catalogues are especially effective with 25-34 age groups, who look to them for inspiration and ideas. This type of cover creates a vision of the better life people might start to enjoy when they buy your products – the art of selling dreams rather than things.

A pure product and
price cover, selling off the page.

A cover showing products but not
selling off the page.

An example of a combination product/lifestyle cover.

A fun example of a fantasy lifestyle cover -
perfect for the brand.

An example of a lifestyle cover with eye contact.

Choosing your front cover products

This is an important decision as the product has to be desirable enough to entice someone to look inside. Plus, products shown on the cover can sell up to three times more than usual, so make sure you have your stock levels prepared.

As a rule of thumb, if your catalogue is going to a cold list of people who have not yet bought, pick a product that has broad appeal and always sells well. Don't worry that this will lead you into a vicious circle where you can only sell a narrow range of best sellers. Just as your website needs a popular product on the home page to get people to stay, so too does your front cover. If it doesn't persuade people to open the catalogue then none of your products stand a chance.

If it's going to be sent to your existing customers, then pick a new product from a popular category. People who have bought from you before look forward to the next catalogue, and are interested to know what new goodies you have. They want you to tempt them with novelty, but it should still be recognisably from the same stable and reinforce your brand.

Choosing your front cover photograph

Whether you go for a product shot, lifestyle image or combination of the two, one big photo is always preferable. Lots of small photos leads to a very 'busy' cover with no real focal point. It's like the difference between a bitty seaside souvenir shop window and a single mannequin in a department store – the latter is so much more alluring.

The exception to the 'one photo' rule is when you have a genuine need to demonstrate that your product range is extremely diverse. Examples might be if you sell furniture, toys and food all from one catalogue, or if you sell products for babies and children of different ages. In instances like these, small inset photos (around three or four maximum) are a good solution, because they tell the story without detracting from the main photo.

▓ Inset photos can be used to show different categories or age ranges.

Inset photos should go at the bottom, horizontally. If you put them in a vertical column the customer reads them as a sort of 'contents list' rather than examples. If you put them at the top, you're in danger of losing your reader's interest before you've even started to get them hooked in on your main photo.

Always write the page number next to the inset photos so that the customer doesn't have to hunt around to find the product inside. If the section covers more than one page, it's more enticing to show just one page number, so instead of "See pages XX-YY" simply write "Starts page XX".

One tip when shooting products for a catalogue cover: ask your photographer to put in a lot more background than they would usually. This gives you an area at the sides to put text without going over the product. It also allows you to use the photos in both portrait and landscape formats. If the photographer crops close you lose that flexibility.

Other front cover elements

The photo gets attention and interest, but other elements are also needed to get people in the mood to buy.

Generally people trust a catalogue more than a website, because they are holding a physical object in their hands. Other cover elements that also build trust include:

- *Your company name and logo* – so people know who you are. Just like a website, it should go at the top, so that customers know straight away where the catalogue has come from. However, don't make it so huge that it dominates the page. Your readers want to know what's in it for them, not all about you!

- *Date or issue number* – such as 'Summer 2011'. This helps keep your catalogue looking fresh and seasonal and is yet another subliminal message to your existing customers that this catalogue is different from the last one with new treats inside.

- *Awards* – If you've won an award this can also be highlighted on the front cover as it helps establish your credibility and authority. People like to buy from winners. Ideally it should go on the left hand side close to the spine, as in eyeflow terms, this is a cold area, and the award can draw the eye over. Often the body that gives the award will supply a smart-looking logo for you to use.

- *'Established since .....' date* – A simple device that helps build trust. Now that we're firmly into the new millennium, all dates starting 19-something (even 1999) are starting to look like they've been around forever. It's very reassuring for your reader to feel that your company has been in business for a long time.

- *Royal warrant* – One of the best marks of trustworthiness for a UK company is a royal warrant, and it makes your products highly desirable. It takes five years of continuously supplying a royal household before you can apply for one. If you're lucky enough to have earned the right to use the coat of arms, never re-draw it. There are strict rules from the Palace not just about colours, design and wording of the legend but also where it has to go on the page (always above or level with your own logo, never below). A royal warrant gets reviewed every year, so don't waste the privilege.

Elements that help position your brand or niche include your logo, corporate design and the style and content of images as well as a:

♦ ***Strapline or tagline*** *– This could be a short phrase and says who you are and what you do or sums up the end benefit of your brand. It is a powerful way to help differentiate your catalogue from your competitors and position your brand in the minds of your customers.*

Elements that work with the photograph and general cover layout to generate interest in the products for sale include:

♦ ***Sub-heads*** *– These short mini-headlines help to give a quick overview of what you are offering and build excitement. A line such as "NEW Organic Chicken Pies" tells new customers that you make foods, and the word 'new' gives existing customers a reason to look inside. Don't worry about putting text on your cover – just make sure it doesn't crowd over the photo too much. Take a look at any magazine shelf and you'll see that the publications are covered in text at the sides - the middle section is reserved for a fabulous photo .*

Finally, elements which encourage the customer to buy include:

♦ ***Phone number and web address*** *– because this says 'here are things for sale' rather than it being a magazine.*

♦ ***Promotion or special offer*** *– This should definitely go on the front cover ideally in the bottom right hand corner. That's because research shows that people read your cover starting at the top left hand corner. The bottom right hand corner, where their eye exits, gives you one final extra chance to persuade them to open your catalogue rather than bin it.*

Respect 'reading gravity' – the natural eyeflow pattern

Cover elements

Designing a catalogue should never be 'painting by numbers' or a formula. We saw earlier how a website has its conventions and so too does a catalogue cover. This basic template has emerged over time as 'best practice' based on research by readability experts such as Colin Whieldon as well as extensive tests by many catalogue marketers. It respects 'reading gravity' – the natural eyeflow pattern that most people follow when they read a single page, starting from the top left hand corner and exiting bottom right. Like the website template earlier, you can break the rules – they are only guidelines, but experience suggests that the end result will be less effective.

Template - catalogue front cover

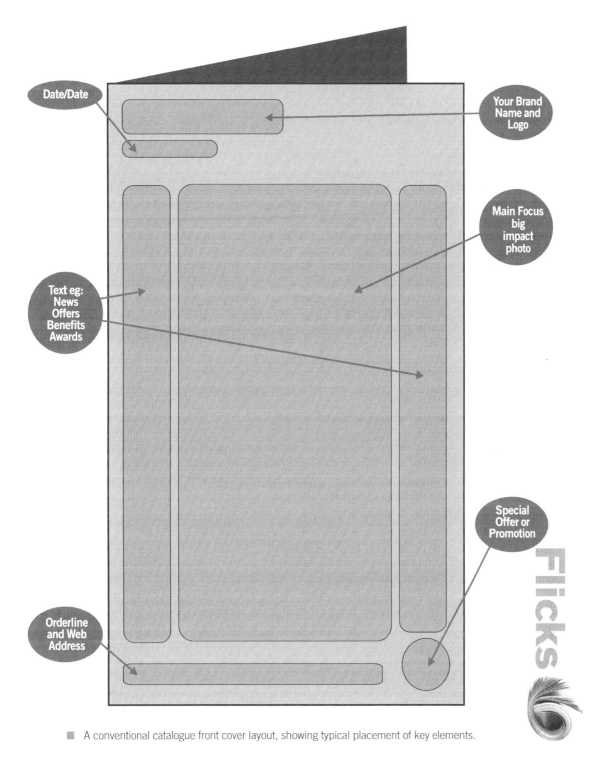

A conventional catalogue front cover layout, showing typical placement of key elements.

Back cover

The back cover is a prime spot that, like the front cover, uplifts sales on any products that you feature here. It could be the first thing your customer sees, as you never know which way up or down the catalogue will land on the doormat. It should have your name and logo so that the reader knows straight away who it's from, and as much 'open-up appeal' as the front cover.

This can be a challenge if it has to incorporate the address panel, which can often dominate the design. Royal Mail regulations are strict about size, colours and placement of the box and it takes up a lot of space. However, you don't need to limit the back cover to one main photo. It can work well to feature three or four products here.

The aim is to present a snapshot of the goods for sale, with products that are representative of the catalogue and the brand. Feature a range of prices, including your most and your least expensive with some in the middle. Always pick your best-selling lines, especially if it's going to prospects, and label each photo with a page number so that potential customers can quickly turn to the products inside.

Inside back cover

A surprisingly large number of people – up to one in three – start flicking through a catalogue from somewhere other than the front cover, according to research. That makes the inside back cover an important hot-spot, so it's worth giving some thought as to what goes here. In an ideal world you would have some juicy, best-selling products, but it's also one of the best places for an order form, if you're using one, as this is where people often expect to find it. To make the most of this prime selling spot, try to make the order form fit onto one page (or less) and leave some space for impulse buys around it. Usually products shown next to an order form get a significant uplift in sales.

If your catalogue is large – say above 1,000 product lines or more, you may need an A-Z index at the back. This is especially true of certain B2B sectors such as nuts and bolts or light bulbs. Try to avoid dense blocks of text in this prime selling spot at the back of the catalogue. Intersperse the list with photos of strategically placed bestsellers or special offers. It all helps to get the reader wanting to look inside.

Spine

Larger catalogues – generally above 48 pages – are too big to be stapled (or 'wire-stitched'). Depending on the thickness of the paper, they can gape rather than lie flat and look rounded on the edges. If your catalogue is produced 'perfect bound' then you'll have a flat area along the spine. It's sometimes called the 'third cover' as it can be used to promote your brand.

These thicker catalogues are often placed on a bookshelf (especially if it's B2B) with only the spine showing. Make yours loud and proud so that your customer can find it quickly.

There are three key elements to get onto the spine – your name, your 5-8 word tagline and your logo or a small element adapted from your logo, sometimes called a 'logo bug'. Design it with high-contrast colours (dark against light and so on) to stand out on the shelf and make your catalogue the one they reach for.

Inside front cover spread (pages 2 and 3)

This is one of the most important spreads in the whole catalogue. It is here that your customer forms their impression of your company and the products. You need to get them in the mood for buying.

This spread is a prime selling space. Indeed, some catalogues go straight into showing products on these opening pages. If you don't do so on your catalogue, it's something you might want to consider. It will certainly increase sales more than if you don't start selling until page five or six.

However, it can build trust and help to increase response if you use a small part of this opening spread to tell your readers something about you. This is where they would generally expect to find information such as:

- *A letter or editorial*
- *Easy 'how to order' options*
- *Symbols and icons legend*
- *Guarantee*
- *Contents / Navigation*
- *Service benefits and delivery information*
- *Other information*

Both existing and potential customers are influenced by this sort of information. Potential customers always have some anxiety about their first purchase and need reassurance, whereas existing customers find it comforting that their favourite company is still as good as it ever was.

Opening letter or editorial

The content of the editorial (usually found on page two) depends on whether or not you are mailing a separate covering letter. When mailing both, the separate covering letter should complement your editorial and not try to compete or repeat. How you do this is by making the separate letter more topical and chatty – like greeting an old friend – whereas the editorial in the catalogue itself has more of a focus on the timeless benefits of the brand and company. It's a tried and tested combination, summed up as "The letter sells the catalogue so the catalogue can sell the products."

However, it may be that you're only mailing the catalogue, either in an envelope or polylope or as a 'naked mailing' with no outer covering. In this case the editorial becomes the only letter so it has to do double duty – the chat and relationship building plus the brand building and what's new.

How to order

The purpose of this section is largely to remind people that you are offering things for sale. It's a simple, yet powerful device which works at a subconscious level to help get people into a buying mood. That's why it's a good idea to show credit card logos here.

The main thing here is not to go into a huge amount of detail (the order form is the place for that) but to simply give topline information – just your phone number and web address, social media icons, and possibly a mention of other methods of ordering. You might want to repeat service benefits here such as 24 hour delivery and free delivery if you offer it.

Also give some thought as to what you call this. "It's easy to order" or "Your shopping list" is a much more inviting headline than "Order Form".

Legend

With space at such a premium in print catalogues, symbols are a great space-saver. Customers tend to expect to find the legend on page 2 or by the order form.

The purist view is that a legend isn't needed as a good symbol doesn't need explaining. A typical 'no smoking' sign is a good example – even a five year old can guess the meaning.

There are some concepts that just don't lend themselves easily to a simple graphic, but symbols can still be useful. The Happy Puzzle Company sells a range of toys, some of which are ideal for children with conditions such as dyslexia. This is highlighted with colour coded dots. Sometimes a symbol can incorporate lettering, like these for Donald Russell to promote its range of oily fish and chef-made dishes respectively.

You can use your legend as another opportunity to build your brand by arranging it in a way that gives a positive impression. Look at your icons and classify them by the type of information they communicate to your customers:

◆ *Benefits (eg: Rich in omega 3)*

◆ *Neutral information (eg: Plant in sunny or partially shaded areas)*

◆ *Negative (eg: Home assembly required)*

◆ *Warning (eg: Not suitable for children under 3)*

Lay out the legend box with the good benefits first. Make them big and bold, and give less prominence to the negative and warning symbols. The aim is not to mislead, but to put the focus on the positives.

Guarantee

Page 2 is an excellent place to display your guarantee. A well crafted guarantee is an easy – and highly under-rated – way to increase sales, for no extra cost. By 'guarantee', I mean some carefully crafted wording and well designed artwork that is part of your corporate identity.

This is sometimes known as a 'brass plaque' or a 'boilerplate' because it is firmly attached in a prominent position to give solid reassurance that you stand by your reputation. It is proof to a potential buyer that you, the seller, are absolutely sure they will be completely satisfied.

Just as with the website it's not enough to write the word "Guarantee" in the same typeface as everything else and hope your customers happen to notice it. Chances are, even if they do spot it in amongst all the rest of the small print, it won't invoke the same instinctive feelings of trust as much as something that's been purposely designed.

■ The same wording, for Laverstoke Park Farm, the organic farm in Hampshire owned by former Formula 1 world champion, Jody Scheckter. Which has more impact?

Guarantees work at a sub-conscious level, which is why archetypal visual devices such as seals, signatures, watermarks and wavy lines are so effective. If you want to see what a great guarantee looks like, simply take any bank note out of your wallet. The design alone says "You can trust me. I am accountable".

You should give as much thought to choosing your wording as your design. A guarantee needs to state clearly what you promise, and it should do it without needing any sort of caveat. A guarantee with an asterisk next to it is no guarantee at all.

Make the guarantee as strong and unequivocal as possible. The ideal is a full, no-quibble, money-back guarantee. Chances are you're offering this anyway, even if it's not formally stated. After all, if an aggrieved customer phones up to complain, you'd probably give them their money back or replace the item, and apologise for causing them inconvenience. If this is your policy, why not capitalise on it?

Of course there are occasions where this just isn't possible, for example if you're offering personalised gifts, made-to-measure pieces such as blinds, or items with hygiene issues such as earrings. In this case, perhaps you could give a 12 month guarantee against defects and workmanship. There's always something you can say to reassure and persuade people to take a chance on you. Just think about how you would handle a real customer complaint and the sort of service you would give as a matter of course.

The other consideration when wording a guarantee is to find something that fits the brand. A 'cast-iron' guarantee is appropriate if you're selling toy cars, but it's not appropriate for soft goods, such as fresh cakes or luxury lingerie.

Wine merchants Davy's are a family-owned company, now run by the fifth generation, with a tradition stretching back to Victorian times. The first suggestion for the title of their guarantee was 'You have my word', but this was rejected as it was recognised that Davy's is a team effort. It was therefore decided to go with 'Our name is your guarantee'.

■ Both the wording and the design of these guarantees are appropriate to the brand and their product sector.

Does the thought of giving a full and unequivocal guarantee make you nervous? Do you fear being left with piles of returns or being bankrupted by refunds? Over the years I've worked with many companies to develop strong guarantees. The reality is that abuse of a guarantee is extremely rare, and it's easy to blacklist repeat offenders.

Any costs are far outweighed by the additional sales that a strong, generous guarantee brings you as well as less tangible benefits such as staff pride. A money-back guarantee works because it stops potential customers falling at the last hurdle. There will always be one or two who get all the way to the point of paying and then waver. Your sincere, well-designed guarantee acts like a balm to soothe their anxious mind and help ease the way to them parting with their cash.

You don't need to convert many waverers into buyers to have a significant uplift in sales.

If the guarantee gives a little extra nudge to just one person in a hundred, and your catalogue response goes up from 2% to 3%, that's a 50% increase in turnover.

This is especially true of first-time purchasers who are taking a big leap of faith by doing business with you. But it's also comforting for your regular customers, who like the reassurance that you still care about them and won't let them down.

Contents/Navigation

If you are going to have a contents section, page 2 or 3 is the place to put it. Of all the elements on the opening spread, the contents list is probably the least important, so make it as short as possible by using broad, generic descriptions, such as 'Footwear' rather than 'Boots' and 'Shoes'. Place it in the middle of the spread rather than the edges as these are the 'hot-spots' better used for selling products.

Be wary of colour coded sections. It may seem logical to have different colours for different types of products – and of course gives you a lovely colourful contents page. However, studies show that people rarely shop by colour in a catalogue (they shop by page number), and it can take five or six visits to a particular section before they even begin to become familiar with them.

Another problem with colour coded sections and contents is that it can create a lot of visual 'noise' especially if you have a lot of sections. If the products you sell are bright and colourful to start with they can just get lost on a background colour. The exception to the rule is holiday brochures, where each colour stands for a geographic region.

However, you may not need a contents list at all if your catalogue has less than 32 pages, as that's generally small enough for people to find their way round easily. Gift catalogues and clothing catalogues can often do without too, as people tend to browse rather than zoning in on something specific. It could be more valuable for your bottom line to get rid of the contents list altogether and use that extra space for another product.

Service benefits and delivery information

Putting your delivery charges on page 2 can help avoid customers being frustrated or disappointed, and also helps to set the mood for buying rather than browsing. Always set out your lowest delivery charges first (rather than lowest order value first – a subtle difference). That means writing:

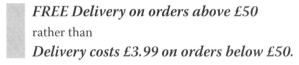

FREE Delivery on orders above £50

rather than

Delivery costs £3.99 on orders below £50.

If returns are free, also mention it.

Service benefits are things such as hemming trousers, free swatch service and free site visits. If you're offering any of these little tit-bits to your customers, let them know, loud and clear on page 2. It all helps to make people feel comfortable about buying from you.

Catalogue pages and double page spreads

You'll notice that I talk a lot about catalogue spreads (meaning double page spread or DPS) rather than pages. That's because the customer always sees two pages at once. The way you design your catalogue spreads makes a big difference to how much you sell.

The specialisation of catalogue design is rarely covered in any depth at graphic design colleges. Most catalogue agencies give their designers additional training which can take several months. As the American catalogue guru Jack Schmid says in his book Creating a Profitable Catalog (sic) "Half the battle is knowing and understanding the rules that enable a catalog to attract attention, tell your product's story, and sell. These rules are not subjective; they represent years of research and testing that demonstrates how consumers read and process information in catalogs."

One of the pioneers of that research is Professor Siegfried Vögele, whose work was so influential that the German Post Office founded and named an institute after him. Vögele eventually developed a whole theory of direct marketing which he called 'dialogue marketing' because it tries to replicate the dialogue that takes place during one-to-one selling.

At the 1986 International Direct Marketing Symposium in Montreux, Vögele unveiled the results of his eye-tracking studies in which volunteers were asked to wear helmets with little video cameras attached while looking at magazines and catalogues. The cameras tracked where their eyes went, a little like the way website heat maps are done today. This insight into how customers view catalogues and advertisements had an immediate impact that still influences catalogue design today.

Eyeflow

Vögele found that, generally, people don't 'read' a catalogue spread from top to bottom, like they might read a newspaper, advertisement or the front cover of a catalogue. Instead, their eye starts on the top right hand corner, skims over to the left hand side briefly, and then shoots off bottom right.

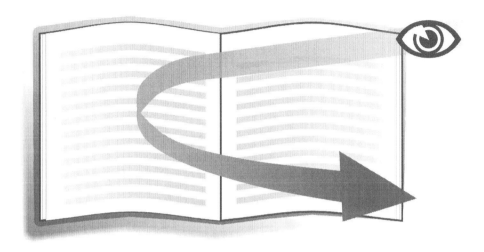

■ The 'Siegfried Line' - the path the eyes naturally follow on a typical catalogue double page spread as discovered through the eye-tracking experiments of Professor Siegfried Vögele.

What this means is that every spread has 'hot-spots' (the areas that the eye will naturally go to) and 'cold-spots' (areas that get skimmed over or not looked at).

■ Hot and cold spots on a typical catalogue spread revealed by eye-tracking studies.

Eye magnets

His research found that typography and images can 'cheat' this natural eye flow to draw the eye to particular areas and thus make better use of the space. The implications are that the left hand page in particular needs some striking visuals to encourage people to glance over. One of the easiest ways is to put a big picture as far to the left as possible. It acts as an 'eye magnet' so that your reader spends more time on all parts of the spread, which gives you more value from every page of the catalogue.

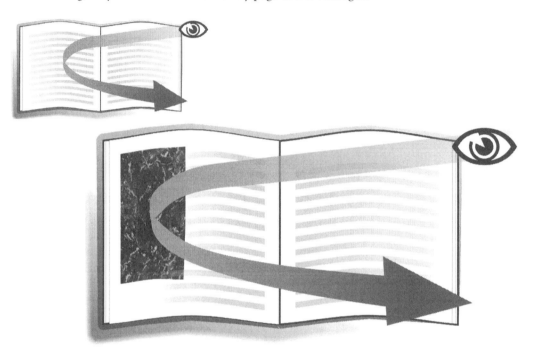

■ Large photographs on the left hand page act as an 'eye magnet' to draw the eye so that the reader looks at more of the spread.

Vögele also studied content, shapes and colours of images to find out which were most effective at attracting the eye. He discovered that there is a natural sequence in which human beings glance at pictures. To make a workable list, he grouped images together in pairs and specified which one is most effective at attracting the eye. Vögele named the stronger images 'amplifiers' as they are like magnets for the eye that can be used to make your reader look at whatever you want them to see and amplify the value of the page.

Interestingly, research conducted in August 2010 by Eyetracker (commissioned by the Royal Mail's Mail Media Centre) showed that our eyes are still drawn towards the same kind of images, suggesting that these eyeflow patterns are as relevant now as they were thirty five years ago.

Those on the right are the 'eye magnets' that always beat those on the left.

EYE MAGNETS	
Vögele's hierarchy of paired images	
Weaker images	**Stronger images**
Resting	**Action shots**
Portrait	**Eye contact**
Full length portrait (whole body)	**Close up portrait** (face)
Adults	**Children**
Single person	**Groups of people**
Objects	**People**
Landscape shapes (horizontal rectangle)	**Portrait shapes** (vertical rectangle)
Square shapes	**Round shapes**
Mid-tones	**Loud colours**
Cold colours	**Warm colours**
Black and white photos	**Colour photos**
Small pictures	**Large pictures**

Vögele hypothesised that this order in which we look at images developed because back in caveman days we needed to scan for danger when we were outdoors, so our eyes would be drawn towards things that could do us harm. A brightly coloured leopard about to pounce is more of a threat than a bush in the distance. The explanation doesn't quite fit for every one of the paired sequences but it's still an interesting theory.

One of the implications for the design of catalogue spreads is to take advantage of natural 'hot-spots' by placing large images (or 'hero shots') in them. Put bestsellers in the hot-spots to attract the reader and keep them reading, or put in new products to add interest for repeat customers.

Careful placement of the visuals (rather than text) on the outside edges is also more likely to attract the attention of the casual reader. When someone is idly flicking through the catalogue rather than opening it up fully their eyes scan the outside edges, so you need eye-catching pictures here (rather than blocks of text) to help to lure them in.

When someone is leafing through a catalogue, they only see the outer edges so place images here to catch the eye and act as landmarks.

It's also helpful for customers who have become familiar with your catalogue as they can find the place they're looking for more quickly. Many consumers look through a catalogue three or four times before they place an order and these hero shots become landmarks that help them lock on to the products they want when they finally decide to buy. It's even more important in business-to-business – consumables like toner cartridges, light bulbs, nuts and bolts and soap refills – when customers may buy several times from the same catalogue.

Naturally, the fact that there are hot-spots also means there are cold-spots. This is where you should put any non-selling information. Lyco, an electrical retailer has a lot of information about different types of light source, such as halogen or LED. These always go in information boxes positioned near the centre of the spread. Donald Russell, a gourmet butcher, does the same with information boxes about the benefits of freezing products or cooking tips.

■ Before: all products the same size.

■ After: electrical retailer Lyco redesigned the catalogue according to Vögele's principles, with 'hero' photos in the hot-spots and information boxes in the cold-spots.

If your product comes in several different sizes and variants (such as greenhouses or picture frames) the cold-spots are the perfect place for a detailed table. Another way to liven up cold-spots is by putting in something to draw the eye, such as the word 'NEW' in a circle in the top left hand corner. This technique also helps to make some spreads look different which adds 'pace' to the catalogue to keep readers turning the pages.

However, the fact is that you can't have every part of the spread highlighted – some spots will always be hotter or colder than others. If everything is 'shouting' then nothing gets heard. The art of a successful catalogue is being aware of eyeflow, hot-spots and cold-spots and using them to your advantage.

Placing copy

When it comes to laying out your photographs and text, you can either:

a) *Place individual copy underneath (or close to) each photograph OR*

b) *Put a key number on each photograph and put all the copy in one block.*

Using key numbers certainly creates a cleaner-looking, less cluttered page, but from the customer perspective (a) makes shopping a lot easier. To demonstrate this, I deliberately wrote the last sentence with (a) in it rather than telling you what the best option is. To find out, you have to go back and remind yourself what (a) means, even though you only read it a few seconds ago.

It's the same with the customer browsing a catalogue. When her eye alights on something she likes the look of, she has to note the code number then find the text it relates to. As I've mentioned before, anything which slows down the customer's path to purchase results in a lower response.

Another problem with having text separate from the photo is that it can be so misleading that people end up ordering the wrong thing. This is either because they mis-read the code number and key number or because they read some text and match it up to the wrong photograph by mistake. It causes bad feeling with your customers, and needless time wasted sorting out the problem.

Footers, headers and page numbers

It's good practice to put the phone number and web address on every single page of your catalogue, ideally in the same place, so that it's really easy to find. Imagine you've got a customer just about to buy and they can't find your address or phone number. While they're hunting to find it, they could so easily get distracted and then you've lost them.

That may sound a bit of an exaggeration, but even if only one person in every three or four hundred people puts your catalogue to one side because they got interrupted while they were looking for your contact details, that's 10% of lost sales (on a mailing with a 3% response rate).

The place your customers look first for the web address and phone number is at the bottom of the spread. Often it's done as a little strip known as a footer, which is a neat way to enclose the contact details without disrupting the design.

Generally it's better to put the web address on the right hand side as it's the more prominent side so helps encourage people to use the web. Alternatively put both the phone number and the web address on the right hand side and use the left hand side for short messages about service benefits such as opening hours, gift wrap or a reminder of the closing date of a special offer.

Some catalogues also have a header, a narrow strip running across the top of the catalogue. Most catalogues benefit from a footer, but few need a header as well. They are generally useful for larger catalogues with extensive ranges of around 500 or more products, with a lot of different categories (eg: indoor lighting) and sub-categories (eg: bathroom lights). They can also be helpful for holiday cottage brochures to help indicate different geographic regions.

Navigation features like this should go at the top, rather than down the side. A vertical strip takes a big slice out of the prime selling space of the catalogue. It also creates a uniform 'bar' look to anyone idly flipping through the catalogue and dilutes the effectiveness of your hero shots.

Page numbers

Page numbers are one of those important little details that can easily be overlooked especially on catalogues with fewer pages. Customers tend to expect to find page numbers on the bottom outside corner. Putting page numbers half way down a page is a waste as they simply don't get noticed

Some catalogues have a graphic style for their page numbers that echoes other elements of the corporate identity like this one (left) for muddy puddles. It's little touches like these that subtly strengthen the brand, give customers confidence and build loyalty.

More products and special offers at www.muddypuddles.com

Order form

The amount of effort that goes into creating a really excellent order form would surprise most people. They look deceptively simple – just a box with spaces for people to fill in what they want. In fact it's one of the most important parts of the catalogue because it's at this point that you are turning an interested reader into a real customer.

The role played by an order form has changed from the days when most orders came through the post with a cheque or postal order. Rather than filling in the order form to tear out and post, customers tend to use it as a shopping list. When they've written down what they want, they then phone up or go online to order, keeping their written record for their own peace of mind.

The order form also plays an intangible psychological role in the selling process by flagging up "Here are goods you can buy" – another way of asking for the sale. It also reassures customers that there is a bricks and mortar business, staffed by real people opening up the postbox in the morning.

Complete order forms

Some order forms list every single item in page order with the price and code. It makes it easy for the customer as all they have to do is write down how many they want of each item.

This rather old-fashioned style of order form stems from the days when people would print one colour catalogue to last all year and have a separate black and white price list. If the prices went up, there was a sale or if something sold out, it was much cheaper to change the price list.

As print technology and customer expectations have changed, this sort of order form is unlikely to increase sales, or justify the extra print and layout costs. Customers are usually happy to fill out the details (and of course very few people post their order form these days). Donald Russell is just one company that made the switch from full list to blank box style order form and found no reduction in response.

Do you need an order form?

Indeed, for some catalogues, it's more profitable to do away with the order form and use the space to sell products. The age group of your customers is the strongest indicator of whether you need an order form, as it's far less important when you're selling to a younger, more web-savvy target audience.

Elements of an order form

The basic information you need on an order form includes:

- *The customer's name and unique customer number or source code and address. It can boost response rates if this information is pre-filled by personalised printing. If so, you'll need to leave enough room for the customer to mark on any corrections.*

- *The customer's email address (remember to leave lots of space as people can have long email addresses. If the order form is narrow then allow two lines putting the @ sign at the start of the second line.)*

- *Space for a delivery address (this can encourage people to buy gifts).*

- *A data protection disclaimer, worded to try and encourage your customer to give permission for them to be contacted with newsletters, future offers and so on.*

- *An address where the order form should be sent.*

- *Space for the products to be ordered. (Allow several lines for this, with columns for page number, product code, description, colour, size, quantity, price each and total price.)*

- *Space to write names etc for personalised products (eg: mug with a name printed on.)*

- *Space for all elements of the credit card, including name on card, tick box to state the billing address is the same as the customer address, expiry date and those three little CCV or security numbers on the back (or four at the front on American Express.)*

In addition, there's lots of other handy information that you might want to put near the order form, such as:

- *Hours of opening for both ordering and customer service. (If you're open 24/7 do say so in big letters – don't assume the customer knows about your fantastic service benefits).*

- *Detailed information about delivery charges.*

- *Product return information.*

- *Legal disclaimers (make these as small and discreet as possible).*

- *Size charts.*

- *Details about products that can be personalised – how many characters and so on.*

The order form is also a great place to ask people to recommend a friend. If you have room, add in a couple of extra 'name and address' boxes and offer a small incentive. It could be your cheapest way of gaining new customers.

It's also an excellent place to suggest add-on purchases that can increase the average order value. If you sell gadgets, offer batteries here. If you sell vacuum cleaners, suggest spare bags.

Order form tips and tricks

As online marketers are discovering in relation to their website checkout processes, an inviting and easy to use order form brings in extra sales. It's well worth spending time and effort to make it work as hard as possible. Here are some design and copy techniques that improve response rates:

1   *Never call it an 'Order Form'. Forms are dull, boring and sound like a chore. It's also unnecessary as it's obvious that it's an order form – you don't need to tell people. Plus, it's also likely that your customers won't actually use it to order but more as a shopping list, so start off with a headline such as "IT'S SO EASY TO BUY", or '"WHAT'S ON YOUR LIST?"*

2   *Use the word 'YES'. It's incredibly powerful. But make sure it's well art-directed so that the YES has the visual power to match the written word. Combine it with reminders of the great benefits of purchasing from you. Write in an active tone of voice, and in the first person, such as:*

"YES. Please send me ____ packets of the life-changing 'Nomor-Aches' wrist chain. I understand that I can try this miracle product for ten days and if I feel so much as a twinge in that time I can return it for a full refund."

If you're offering free delivery or a free gift, use the bottom line of the grid to remind them of it, using similar first person wording:

"YES: My order totals £50 or more. Please send me my free gift worth £10."

"YES: I am ordering before (date), so I qualify for FREE DELIVERY."

3   *If you can, make your order form time-limited. Again this is probably more suited to a mail order advertisement than a catalogue, but the principles still apply. A time-limited offer gives a sense of urgency to make your customer feel they have to do it now. That's important because if they don't act now, a lot of them never will.*

4   *If your product has a complex purchasing process (for example, if it requires taking measurements), then keep these instructions separate from the order form. They could, for example, go on the left hand side of the spread, with the order form on the right. Simplify the process down into easy step-by-step directions and use cheery graphics to make it look easy and fun.*

59

4 *A very effective design trick is to put a tint behind all parts of the order form except those you want the customer to fill in, such as their name and address. At a glance, the customer can see what they have to do, and it gives an impression that there's less to fill in. Although it's a time-consuming design process, it makes the order form look clean and neat, and above all, easy.*

5 *Include reassuring messages on or near the order form. This is the time you can lose customers simply because they get cold feet so try and do everything you can to make them feel comfortable. It's always a leap of faith to buy something, especially if it's a first time purchase. Visuals such as your guarantee, the SHOPS (Safe Home Ordering Protection Scheme) symbol and credit card symbols all help to reduce risk and break down the barriers to buying.*

6 *Relevant testimonials from customers encourage the customer to buy. Rather than yet more glowing quotes about the products, try to find a quote for here that praises an aspect of delivery or after-sales service, such as how fast the parcel arrived or how quickly and efficiently a problem was sorted out. (Don't be nervous about mentioning something slightly negative. If the testimonial shows the problem was dealt with fast and the customer had no hassle, it sends out a very powerful message.)*

7 *If you want to encourage people to order online put your web address in big letters. Remind them of the benefits such as 24 hour shopping, web-only specials and instant stock information. Make it easy to see the phone number as this is reassuring, but make your postal address tiny to discourage ordering by mail.*

8 *Use the small print to your advantage. Almost every order form needs a certain amount of small print either on it or nearby. Small print is bad news as it puts customers off. They assume it's all negative, so do everything you can to dispel this notion.*

This is how you do it. Firstly, go through and see which bits of the small print are beneficial for the customer. For example, most order forms show the delivery charges, but many companies offer free delivery over a certain spend. Turn this around to be a benefit for the customer by leading on the free delivery, for example:

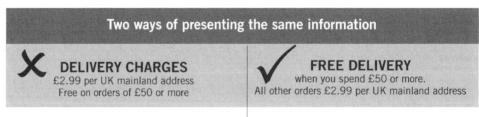

Two ways of presenting the same information	
✗ DELIVERY CHARGES £2.99 per UK mainland address Free on orders of £50 or more	**✓ FREE DELIVERY** when you spend £50 or more. All other orders £2.99 per UK mainland address
This version hides the benefit of free delivery and uses the negative word 'charges'.	A positive message with the powerful word 'FREE' to attract attention.

Look carefully at every other single piece of small print on your order form and try to turn negatives round to a positive. Instead of 'Parcels must be returned within 14 days' say 'You have 14 days to return your parcel.' Make everything sound as simple and easy as possible.

When you have designed your order form, ask someone to fill it in as if they were a customer. It's the best way to spot any glitches, such as whether you've left enough space for someone to fill in their name and address, credit card details and so on. Phone the telephone number to make sure it works. (I say this as someone who has twice signed off advertisements with the wrong phone number in them. Not the most glorious moments of my career.) It's so tempting to skip this step, yet it almost invariably throws up something blindingly obvious that somehow got overlooked.

Summary

Your catalogue cover is your shop window. Elements that make up a good cover include a great photo, your company name and logo, strapline and incentives to open the catalogue such as an offer or a message about new products. A web address and orderline phone number establishes that this is a catalogue with things for sale.

Your back cover is a prime selling spot, so show best-selling products that give a flavour of the catalogue and make people want to look inside.

If you have a flat spine, remember to use it to promote your brand.

Catalogues are designed in spreads (of two pages) rather than single pages. Use hero shots in the hot-spots, and text, grids and diagrams in the cold-spots.

Put the phone number and web address on every page.

If you have an order form, design it with care to encourage ordering.

3 | **Anatomy of a catalogue**

4 | How to plan your catalogue pages

The internet has changed the way catalogues are planned. Before websites existed your catalogue was your store, and had to contain every single product. If it wasn't in the book, it wouldn't sell. This meant that the planning always started with the products, with the task being to work out the minimum number of pages needed to fit them all in.

Today, when the catalogue no longer has to represent your entire range, it has become a device to promote the store. With no need to show every product in every variation, the planning of catalogues has changed. It now starts with the size and shape, and the trick is to work out the best products to fit the pages.

In both cases, the three vital elements are space, pace and place.

Space – choosing size and format

A key decision to be made at the start is the dimensions of your catalogue. Ever since the Royal Mail brought in Pricing in Proportion (PIP) there has been a huge financial incentive to produce catalogues smaller than 240mm x 165mm – just a little over A5 – as this size falls into a cheaper price band, so can cost less to post.

Choosing a format

It's at this point that you also need to choose your format - portrait, landscape or square. The most widely used format is portrait, because it's easy to read and easy to handle. Landscape and square formats are more unusual, so can help you stand out. However, it can be harder to design to take advantage of eyeflow.

A landscape double page spread is a long, wide shape, and the eye can only scan from side to side. It's also an awkward shape to show products that are naturally tall and narrow, which includes most fashions (dresses, trousers) and household items (cutlery, mugs, jugs, floor lamps, mops, vases, fridges and so on).

However, landscape can work really well where you have naturally wide products such as designer mats, sports cars or a row of wine bottles, so be guided by the shape of the majority of your merchandise.

■ A landscape format suits products like designer doormats and cases of wine, which are naturally short and wide in shape. Most other products, such as fashion (above) are naturally tall and narrow in shape and suit a portrait format catalogue.

Choosing the number of pages

Having decided on a page size and format, the next question is how many pages? This partly depends on whether you have a requirement to feature a given number of products. If so, your task here is to work out how to get that number to fit neatly into the spreads, with sufficient space for each product.

As a rule of thumb, allow two or three high to mid-priced products per page and around four to six for lower priced products. How you define the 'higher' or 'lower' priced depends on your business. It also depends on the type of products, how much explanation they need, and the degree of emotional involvement the customer is likely to have. For example, a sewing machine will always need more space than a needle and thread.

However, these are only guidelines for product density - there are no hard and fast rules. It's a question of judgement, compromise and common sense. The idea is to get to a point where you've reached a workable compromise between the number of products, the size and the number of pages. Remember that the pages always go up in multiples of four.

The other way is to start with a budget for your catalogue and fix the number of pages you can afford. This is often how 'bestsellers' catalogues for prospects start out. In this case your task is the other way round – you're choosing products to fit into the space available. Again, you should allow around six to ten per spread, depending on the type of products and size and format of the pages.

Whichever is your starting point, the next step is to start working out which products go on which page by creating a flatplan – the framework on which your catalogue will be built.

Place and pace – creating a flatplan

The term flatplan comes from the publishing industry, where it's used as a blueprint for magazines from start to finish. It's one of the hidden secrets of successful catalogues and it saves huge amounts of time, hassle and money as well as making the finished catalogue look better and perform better.

Without a flatplan, producing a catalogue is a bit like going on a car journey with only a sat nav. You have the instructions to get you there, but if you take a wrong turn you won't know until you're in the ditch or on the wrong side of the motorway. The flatplan is a map that lets you see the whole route at once.

In its simplest form, a flatplan is a grid that shows an overview of the products, editorial and offers on each double page spread. It looks a little like a list in a grid format, yet that simplicity belies what a powerful planning tool a flatplan is. A list does not let you see at a glance how the whole catalogue fits together. The flatplan is used in conjunction with a list as a rock solid foundation for everything that follows and allows you to:

- *Get a good balance of products on the page*
- *Group products together into customer-friendly themes*
- *Group the themes together into easily navigable sections*
- *Find a logical flow through your catalogue*
- *Take advantage of the 'hot-spots', and enhance the 'valleys'*
- *Plan your offers and allow space for them*
- *Avoid bottlenecks and jumbles*

Rather like the process for planning a web structure, there are four steps to creating a catalogue flatplan:

1 **Listing:** *List all your products.*

2 **Grouping:** *Group your products into similar areas (from the customer point of view).*

3 **Allocating:** *Allocate the products to spreads, indicating hero products.*

4 **Filling in the flatplan and fine tuning:** *Fill in the products on the flatplan diagram. Review the flow and make any final adjustments. Also add in other information such as introductions, editorial, information boxes, diagrams and call-outs.*

A Flatplan for a 68-Page Catalogue Selling Fountains, Ponds and Water Features

Back Cover / Front Cover	2-3 Welcome/ Overview of categories/ Bestsellers	4-5 Self contained water features	6-7 Self contained water features	8-9 Plumbing/ Designing a water garden
10-11 Water garden kits	12-13 Water garden kits	14-15 Water feature projects	16-17 Planning/Designing a fish pond	18-19 Fish kits
20-21 Fish kits	22-23 Fish kits	24-25 Koi kits	26-27 Koi kits	28-29 Liners
30-31 Liners	32-33 Waterfalls	34-35 Pumps	36-37 Pumps	38-39 Hoses Filters Fittings
40-41 Filters	42-43 Filters	44-45 Filters	46-47 Filters Maintenance Filter Media	48-49 Vacuums and cleaners
50-51 Nets/gloves/waders Deterrents	52-53 Electrical	54-55 Chemicals	56-57 Chemical Food	58-59 Food
60-61 Air pumps	62-63 Lighting	64-65 Glossary and detailed info about calculating a pond size	66-67 Impulse Buys Order Form	

■ This is a very simple flatplan used in the early stages for planning flow and themes. Later versions included the names of each product as well.

Step 1 – *Listing*

Just like when planning a website, the first stage is a list. However, while you can start planning a website structure with a list of just the product names, the catalogue list needs to be much more detailed. Try to have as much information about each product as possible so that when you start allocating products to spreads, you can make judgements about how much space each one needs. This is the kind of information to include on your list:

- *Product Name*
  (exactly as it will appear in the catalogue and on your website)

- *Manufacturer's name (if different)*
  - *Including this will avoid confusion, and make sure the right photos are matched up to the right text*

- *Product code*

- *Price*

- *Quantity*
  - *Eg: weight, number in a pack*

- *Sizes*

- *Dimensions*

- *Delivery issues*
  - *Eg: personalised item, heavy item, self-assembly required*

- *Colours*

- *Is it new to this catalogue?*

- *Is it exclusive?*

- *If it's not exclusive, is it unusual, hard-to-find or some kind of speciality?*

- *Is it a bestseller?*

- *Key information*
  - *Eg: materials, functions, sales literature*

- *Photo brief*
  - *Do photos exist?*
  - *Are they from the supplier or specially shot?*
  - *Is there a choice of photos?*
  - *If photos need to be taken, when will this take place?*

The list should be a regarded as a reference manual, with all the information needed for each product in one place. It needs to be easily at hand when anyone in the team is working on a particular page.

Step 2 – Grouping

Once your list is ready, the next step is to group your products together into similar themes. Try to do this from the customer point of view. If you buy in products from a number of suppliers, or have them made in different factories, you might find that products that a consumer would think were similar are completely separate on your own list.

Say you sell croquet sets and some are crafted from wood and others are made from plastic. From an operational viewpoint, wooden toys and plastic toys are quite different. To the customer, they're the same and potential buyers prefer to see them together so they can compare the price and quality.

Keep the customer in mind

At this stage, all you are doing is grouping your products together into similar types. Sometimes people like to do this with cards or stickers, a little like when working out website classifications. Other people use highlighter pens to mark up the lists. However you do it, always be guided in your choices by how the customer sees the product groups.

After the first sort, you may want to go back and split out some of the larger groups into smaller ones, and possibly put some of the smaller groups together as one, to even out the numbers. However, don't force this just for the sake of neatness – always keep in mind how the customer will see the products.

Step 3 – Allocating

Having sorted your list into groups, the next stage is to allocate them to spreads. It's important to know the prices and how much each product sells as a percentage of the total turnover. You can then give a lot of space to products that sell well, have a high value or have particularly good margins.

Make sure your new products are not all grouped at the back. Conventional wisdom says you should put your flagship products early on as these are the most popular, but you do need new products spread throughout the catalogue to keep the interest going for your loyal repeat customers.

If you sell childrenswear, always start with the younger ages. If parents see a baby, they will usually flick through to find items for older kids, but if a teenager is on the front cover, people with babies won't even look.

Try to keep in mind your brand personality, and give priority to those that support it best. However, many catalogues have some 'opportunist' products – things that aren't a pure fit with the brand positioning, but appeal to the customers and sell well. Because they can dilute the brand, try to place them in the middle pages (but not the centre spread – one of the catalogue hot-spots as it tends to fall open easily so is usually seen more than other spreads).

Squinch analysis

This rather odd-sounding technique is short for 'Square Inch Analysis'. By comparison with Google Analytics, it's a rather low-tech affair, involving a clear screen marked with a grid ten squares across and ten squares down. This is placed onto the page and products are given a score depending on how many squares each one occupies. This is then compared with how much revenue each product brings, using some rather complex calculations. Next time around, the star performers are given a bit more space in the catalogue while those that don't sell so well are given less space or even kicked out.

In theory the catalogue then becomes more attractive to customers and more profitable. However, detractors say that it can rip the soul out of a catalogue, reducing an essentially creative process to a sort of 'painting by numbers'. They also point out that giving less space to non-selling elements (such as lifestyle photographs) can depress sales overall.

Squinch has also been behind controversial marketing decisions, such as taking out a product that helps another one to sell. Where there are three similar products representing good, better and best, the middle price/value product will always sell the most, but to achieve stellar sales it needs the other two to act as foils. When they are removed sales can fall dramatically, reducing the total ROI of the entire page.

Squinch analysis is used mainly on 'big book' catalogues and is becoming less widely used nowadays. However it's still a useful way of looking at things and helping to decide which products to feature as the hero.

Give a lot of space to products that sell well

Placing the products

Creating a flatplan is an art as well as a science, so use your judgement to get a good balance of price points, bestsellers and 'product density' (quantity of products on a page). During the planning you'll probably find that some spreads fall very nicely into place. The groups you put together at the start turn out to contain just the right number of products to sit neatly onto one or more spreads. Others, however, will be more tricky and need a bit of juggling.

Highlight on the flatplan your best-selling, high margin products, as these are candidates to be 'heroes', with a big photo and extra copy. Heroes need to be well spread throughout the catalogue to keep the pace going and your reader continually interested to keep turning the pages.

Pace

Pace is a quality ascribed to catalogues that have a lot of variety and interest, which helps to draw in the reader and keep them turning the pages. Although it's largely down to the design, it's quite helpful to think about pace at this stage and have it in mind when drawing up the flatplan.

Here are some ways to achieve catalogue pace, although try not to use them all at once, or your catalogue will look a mess! Make sure everything is within your corporate design guidelines, to protect your brand identity.

- *Use a variety of photos – close ups and long shots, products and people, indoors and outdoors*
- *Vary the photo shapes, with squares, circles and cut-outs.*
- *Mix blocks of text with text that's wrapped around the copy*
- *Use two or three different grids or templates for the layout to build in variety*
- *Experiment with white backgrounds and coloured backgrounds*
- *Vary the amount of space around your products, giving more 'air' to your expensive items*
- *Add something unexpected and different.*
- *Introduce 'stopper pages'. This simply means starting a new category on a right hand page (instead of starting it on the left hand page of a double page spread). This works particularly well where you have some products that straddle two categories. For example, if your categories are indoor lights and outdoor lights, you may have some that can be used both indoors and outdoors.*

In addition you can use graphic devices to draw attention to particular products, such as:

- *Icons to highlight special features*
- *Starbursts, roundels, rosettes and flashes. (eg: New, Exclusive, Bestseller, Great Value, Free Delivery. Yes, I know, it sounds tacky. But they are very effective and in the hands of a good designer they can be tasteful!)*
- *Information boxes with tips, recipes, facts and background information; "Did you know?" and "Have you seen?" etc.*
- *Call-outs (arrows pointing to specific features on a photograph or diagram)*
- *Testimonials from customers, experts or journalists as well as product reviews from magazines or even your own website.*
- *Quotes from journalists*

Step 4 – *Filling in the flatplan and fine tuning*

The final step is to take a blank grid and write in which products are going on to which spread. First of all mark elements that are in fixed positions, such as the order form, contents and guarantee. Then add the products. It's a bit like doing a crossword puzzle or a Sudoku.

You can do the first draft on PowerPoint, on specialist flatplan software or even by hand with a pencil and eraser. If you're creating your own PowerPoint table, mark up the first box as 'back cover', the second box as 'front cover' and the first spread as 'pages 2-3'. That way it relates to the way the pages will be designed and go to the printer. The odd numbers are always on the right hand side of each spread.

Blank flatplan - for a 24 page catalogue

Project ———————————— Version ———————————— Date ————————

Back Cover	Front Cover	2 - Intro - Contents - Guarantee	3	4	5
6	7	8	9	10	11
12	13	14	15	16	17
18	19	20	21	22	23 - Order Form - Recommend a Friend form

If you have several ranges of similar products, place them in price order starting with the most expensive. The better photo and features attract attention and get the reader interested, then they trade down to the mid-priced option. If you start with the low priced version it's much harder to get your reader to trade up.

As you start to transfer your list of groups onto the flatplan, you'll start to get a feel for whether there are the right number of products on each page, and whether the themes and flow are working. Try to keep the names of the products the same as on the list to avoid confusion within the team.

This is where the real value of the flatplan reveals itself to you, as it's easy to spot all kinds of areas that can be improved. You can now move products around – or add an extra two spreads (four pages) so that it all fits together. It's so much better to make these kind of amends now, rather than when the catalogue is in the studio, where every change costs money.

Before you start production, you might think about asking for comments from everyone on your team including the art director and copywriter. Sometimes a fresh pair of eyes spots a potential problem or an opportunity. Try, if you can, to present the flatplan. Talking people through it means you're more likely to get useful suggestions.

Making changes to your flatplan

Changes are often made, as products come in or out of stock, for example. If you change the format from, say, A4 to A5 or from landscape to portrait, do a new flatplan to check the flow still works.

Make sure to put the latest date and version number on these revised flatplans and keep everyone on the team informed so they know exactly which one to work from. It's always much cheaper and easier to change a flatplan than finished artwork. This groundwork shows itself in a much better organised and effective catalogue when it finally goes to press and better sales when it drops through the letterbox.

Summary

Flatplans are the hidden secret of successful catalogues. A flatplan is an overview, with a page-by-page summary of products. It's a valuable planning tool, that acts as a blueprint or map for catalogue production.

Choose your page size, format and number of pages first. Size and number of pages will be governed by your budget and the number of products you have to include. Format will be influenced by the shape of the products.

There are four stages to creating a flatplan, Listing, Grouping, Allocating, and Filling in and fine tuning.

Use your flatplan to plan the space, pace and place of your catalogue. Ask for comments on the final flatplan from your team before work starts, and always update the version number to avoid confusion.

4 | **How to plan your catalogue pages**

5 | Branding

How powerful is a brand?

The answer is, powerful enough to persuade not one, but two people, to buy a product costing £87,000 – from nothing more fancy than a mailing pack sent through the post.

Drayton Bird, author of Common Sense Direct & Digital Marketing, tells the story of how, in 1981, a mailing was sent out in conjunction with the Automobile Association (itself a hugely well established and trusted brand) offering a car for sale. Two people bought one. Of course, they weren't just buying any old car; they were buying a Bentley, another very powerful and well-known brand.

It's easy to think of the world's giant brands – Coca Cola, MacDonald's, Nike, Microsoft and so on – and assume that (a) branding is for huge multinationals and (b) it's all about having a good logo. Both of these assumptions are wrong.

Branding for catalogues and websites

The principles of branding are just as effective – in fact, essential – for catalogues and websites. A brand helps to future-proof your business. However, creating a brand does take vision and will which has to come from someone senior within the organisation – ideally a board member. And it doesn't stop there. Once the brand is developed it needs to be nurtured and maintained.

It is worth the effort as branding acts as a shortcut to trust and understanding and has a huge influence on what customers decide to buy and how much they are prepared to pay. On the next page are lots more benefits of owning a strong brand.

Why branding is important

- In a world of consumer choice a brand is the only difference that makes you unique
- It builds trust as it represents a 'promise kept' that allows customers to shop with confidence
- It helps to keep your customers loyal
- It makes your business more resilient in the tough times
- It helps achieve higher growth
- It's a key business asset protected in law
- It helps you get a higher price

David Nieper is one of Britain's most successful home shopping companies. It is a true British fashion house, designing and selling exquisite nightwear that sells for four or five times the price of a High Street nightdress. Managing Director Christopher Nieper puts this down to years of building a strong brand, consistently communicating the benefits and maintaining quality levels in both product and service. As he says, "The whole point of a brand is that you can get a premium price for your product".

What is a brand?

There's a lot of mystique around branding. Everyone can name brands, and we all think we know one when we see it. However, very few people have first hand experience of brand creation and management as practised by classical branded goods manufacturers like Unilever, Mars, Kellogg's or Proctor & Gamble.

Even trying to define a brand is confusing because the word 'brand' is used to mean several different things:

a) *In everyday use it is simply the name of a product or service (eg: "Which brand of soap powder do you use?")*

b) *In a legal sense it can mean a trademark. (eg: Ibuprofen marketed under the brand name Nurofen).*

c) *In accounting, the brand is sometimes given a value as one of the assets of a business, even though there is nothing tangible to show for it, such as a factory.*

d) *It can be used to refer to the brand umbrella or to endorse individual products (eg: Kellogg's Rice Krispies, the breakfast cereal and Rice Krispies Squares, the biscuits made of Rice Krispies).*

e) *Finally, there is brand equity, the beliefs, expectations or personality around products and services by a particular company or sold under a particular brand name (eg: "The strike is really going to hurt the British Airways brand").*

However, the true essence of a brand is neatly summed up in a recent Kellogg's TV commercial as "A trusted sign of quality".

History of Brands

Brands began around the time of the industrial revolution. Prior to that, people had lived close enough to where the products were made that they knew and trusted the maker or the seller. As the distance between the production of goods and the point of sale grew, it became important for buyers to know who they were buying from. Manufacturers started to develop marks and symbols that could easily be recognised so that customers would favour their goods over an unmarked product.

It's no coincidence that so many of the early brand marks – Kellogg's, Boots, Mars, Cadbury's and so on were originally a signature. It makes contracts legally binding so it's the ultimate sign of trust and accountability. As time went on brands became more sophisticated, with every communication with customers having the same graphic look and tone of voice.

It was apparent from a very early date that the power of the brand is the trust it inspires in your customers. The value of a brand was also recognised from an early date as this quote shows:

> *"If this business was split up and I would give you the land and bricks and mortar and I would take the brands and trademarks, then I would fare better than you."*

John Stuart, Chairman of Quaker (c. 1900)

Over one hundred years ago, it was understood that customers are deeply – and irrationally – attached to their favourite brands. When leading brands, including Heinz Baked Beans and Coca Cola, are put into blind taste tests, it's often a competitor that comes out on top. However, as soon as the labels are shown, people prefer the brand they know. That's because, when it comes to selling, emotions always trump reason.

How to create your own brand

Your brand is the integration of your products, your culture, your reputation and your brand personality in the minds of the consumer.

The best brands are born out of something real and authentic about your business. Why do you do what you do? (Sometimes known as your 'Core Purpose'). How does your business make the world a better place? (Sometimes known as your 'Higher Order Benefit'). What makes you different?

Another way of looking at it is:

- *Who we are*
- *What we do*
- *Why it matters*

A common mistake is to think that your logo is your brand. It's exciting and fun designing a new logo, so it gets a lot of attention from all sorts of people within the company. However, your logo and the graphic devices are simply the visual signs that represent your brand. It's what those graphics represent that's important.

Another mistake with branding is to over-complicate it. It's very easy to get carried away with brand wheels and fancy diagrams, but if you can't communicate simply what your brand stands for, in words a five year old can understand, then there's little hope of ever getting through to your customers.

Some brands have mastered the art of simplicity to such a degree that their brands can be summed up in just one word:

Coca Cola – *Refreshment*
Volvo – *Safety*

Of course, there is far more to the brand than just the single word, but the fact that they can be so simply and credibly pigeonholed indicates just how strong those brands are, and how consistently they have been applied for decades all over the world.

Branding in catalogues and websites

A lot of the best known brands are owned by global marketing companies with huge budgets, so how can the principles be applied to catalogues and websites?

The fact is, it's not the size of a brand that's important but the clarity of thinking and consistency across every part of the organisation. Brands add value, and the home shopping businesses that build a brand will do better and survive longer than those that don't.

Davy's is a traditional London wine merchants and runs about thirty winebars and restaurants in London. When we were developing the brand, we went through the exercise of looking at what is at the heart of the company. It operates in two highly competitive sectors, especially the retail wine operation. What makes Davy's different? It is a family owned company with a long heritage – the firm was founded in 1870 and is one of the oldest surviving independent wine merchants in Britain.

But how does all this translate through into a benefit for the customer who can buy good quality wine from many different places? After much debate, we came to the conclusion that no other wine merchants make the same choices about which wines to stock. Davy's wine buyers have specific ideas about what makes a truly excellent wine. As a small, private company they have the freedom and the integrity to buy the wines they enjoy and believe others would too. It's not just about good wine – that's a given – it's about choosing good wines that, in the opinion of Davy's, offer something special.

In other words, the Davy's brand can be summed up in one word, 'judgement'. This brand value – together with the brand constant that wine is at the heart of Davy's – is interwoven into every marketing communication Davy's creates. It's integral to their guarantee, the website and every piece of communication.

Another successful e-commerce brand is Muddy Puddles, the UK market leader in children's rainwear. Yet the company doesn't see itself as a purveyor of miniature-sized macs. When I first started working with the founder, Susie Cullen, we defined the higher order benefit as 'protection'. Susie lives on a working farm and she founded the company when she couldn't find decent protective clothing for her children, so she made her own.

Waterproof all-in-ones are still the core product, but as the company expanded into other areas it came to stand for almost any sort of clothing that would protect children, including sun products, and skiwear. In a wider sense, the clothes were also about protection of innocence from the modern world, by providing practical, reliable clothing, uninfluenced by fashion, a look that was entirely consistent with the truth about the farm location and the history of the company.

Brands don't have to stay still, and later on the brand was developed to encompass 'adventure', which is the 'higher order benefit' of protection. From the very start, it was obvious the company was not selling waterproof suits but the happy rosy-cheeked smile of a child who has just spent all morning outdoors playing.

But what if potential buyers are turned off by the idea of 'protection' or 'everyday adventure'. What if they don't agree that a wine merchant has a unique judgement that's special and rare? Isn't it dangerous to exclude lots of potential buyers?

In fact, failing to appeal to everyone is a necessary part of building a strong brand. When you target a specific group of customers there will always be some that you'll miss out on. However, the people you do attract will be far more loyal because you've given them iron-clad reasons to be with you.

When and how do you communicate your brand?

The concept of a brand means that it is integral to everything you do like letters through a stick of rock. It becomes formed in your customers' minds not by what you say but by what you do. That's why your message needs to be clear and consistent every time you interact with your customer – all the touchpoints.

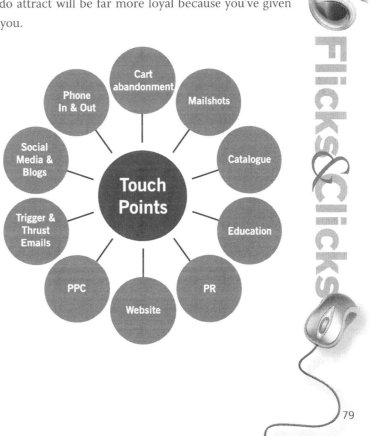

■ Typical customer touchpoints.

Summary

Branding is one of the most powerful ways to add value, improve sales and protect your business in the long term.

A brand is not just your logo, it's your entire reputation, brand identity and personality in your customer's mind.

The easiest and most effective way to develop a brand positioning, personality and identity is to root it in some fundamental truth about your business.

Your brand needs to be consistent across the board, and be reflected in your products, packaging, pricing, attitude to customers, approach to dealing with queries and complaints as well as the tone of voice and visual look of all your communications.

5 | **Branding**

6 | **Principles of copywriting**

There's a lot of mystery and myth surrounding copywriting, as though it's some kind of magical art that only a few, naturally gifted people are able to do. The reality is a lot more down to earth. The two most important things you need to know to brief, write and judge effective copy are your product and your customer.

The role of copy

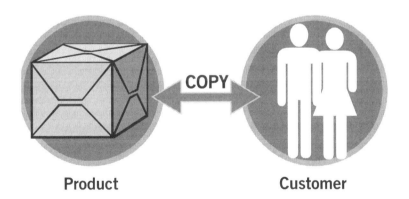

Product   **Customer**

◼ Copy is the message about one to the other.

Copy is simply the message about one to the other, written in the most compelling way possible. Some of the best copy is written by company owners such as Heather Gorringe of Wiggly Wigglers, Angus Thirlwell of Hotel Chocolat or the eponymous David Nieper. It reads as if they were speaking to someone right there in front of them and all the focus is on what the products will do for the customer, not how great the company is.

They write great copy because they can vividly picture their customer and they know the products inside out. Whether you're writing the copy yourself or if you're involved in briefing and approving it, you need to aim for the same levels of passion, insight and product knowledge. Luckily there are techniques you can use to gain an intimate understanding of your customer and quickly learn all the salient features of the product.

Getting close to your target audience

It's very easy to lose sight of individual customers when your call centre and website are taking in hundreds or thousands of orders every month. To analyse the business

and make decisions, it's necessary to bundle groups of people together according to criteria like what they buy and how often and how much they spend. They get given descriptions like buyers, multi-buyers, enquirers, prospects, or even code names like T1's. This is great for analysis, but not great for creativity.

To get close to your customer it is essential to forget about the thousands and focus on one individual. Start with a description of your target audience. You'll probably have a good idea already from research, lifestyle profiling, postcode analysis, feedback from the call centre, or simple common sense based on the type of products you sell.

Profiling your customer

Think about their favourite films and TV shows, their best ever holiday, the car they drive, or who they would invite to their dream dinner party. If you know what sort of magazines and newspapers they read, pick up a copy, and also download a media pack. They're full of valuable psychographic insights into your customers. The Telegraph, for example, gives pen portraits and photos for six different types of reader including "Living The Dream: Switched-on and savvy professionals with diverse interests and a broad outlook" and "Discerning Indulgers: Middle-aged and older individuals, modest and frugal."

Try to visualise what someone in your target audience might look like. Next, shut your eyes and picture yourself as a fly on the wall in that person's home. (If you're in the B2B sector picture that person's workplace instead.) Simply observe, and don't judge. It's important that you like and respect your customers, otherwise it's impossible to sell to them. Mentally watch them as they go about their daily business and take note of the following:

◆ *The phone rings and it's someone they speak to every few days or more.*
  Who might they be and what are they talking about? Who else does your
  customer speak to on a regular basis?

◆ *Have a look at the mantelpiece. What is displayed there? Name at least three objects. (If B2B, substitute 'desk' or 'workspace' for 'mantelpiece'.)*

◆ *They have a drink. What is it? Perhaps it's a cup of tea, a mug of coffee, a cold drink or something else. What are they drinking it from?*

◆ *Something has happened to make them cross. It could be a memory, something on the TV, or perhaps a letter or an article in the paper. What is it and why has it angered them?*

Could you see your customer? This is an exercise that I often do on my copywriting workshops, and I'm constantly amazed at the vivid detail people see in these imaginary scenarios. The pictures and ornaments on the mantelpiece are so real they could almost reach out and touch them. One person said, "She's drinking Earl Grey out of an Emma Bridgewater mug" as if they could actually smell the fragrant tea.

The point about this is that it doesn't matter whether you're right or wrong. If you can picture your customer this well, you have understood the essence of truth about your customer which will let you connect with them when you start to write the copy.

Make your customer real

The final step is to give this customer a real identity. Think of someone you know who could be the person you were imagining in their home or office. Who are they? Can you name them? By this I don't mean calling them 'Trixie' or 'Poppy', but to think of a real live person, and making them your honorary customer.

It could be someone you've met just once, (as long as you spent some time talking to them), it could be a family member, or it could even be yourself, if you fit the target audience. The key thing is that they represent a typical customer, and that you feel you know them enough to be able to strike up a conversation with them. The reason for identifying this one customer is this:

Whenever you write copy, always write for one person.

This is the single most important piece of advice I can give you. Imagine them in the room with you. What would you say to them? Or pretend you are writing them an email or a letter. If it helps you to get going, start off by writing 'Hi' or 'Dear' followed by their name. You can always edit that out later.

Let yourself go and focus your mind on this one person. Don't worry about your hundreds or thousands of other customers. If you can write with conviction to the individual, you will pull in all the other potential customers like a magnet, but if you try and write for everyone, you'll please no-one. The only thing you have to do is remember to take a look later and check that you've said nothing that will actually alienate a core section of your customers.

Interrogating your product

The other part of your copywriting preparation is to learn as much as you can about the object you are writing about. When multi-national companies create ads they spend months interrogating the product. In my agency days I was always off on factory visits to see ice cream being made or talking to the scientists who were working on the latest hair removal cream.

In the world of home shopping, where there are dozens, or hundreds of products needing copy – often in a hurry – it's rare to get that luxury. Time and money constraints mean that copy often has to be written from just a photograph and a briefing sheet. However, if you have any opportunity to work from the product itself, the resulting copy will be much more powerful.

Interrogating the product means being as imaginative as possible about trying to find out things about it. Ask questions.

- ♦ *Where was it made?*
- ♦ *How was it made?*
- ♦ *How long was the production process?*
- ♦ *What are the ingredients?*
- ♦ *Who invented the recipe or the formula?*
- ♦ *How long has the factory been making these kinds of goods?*
- ♦ *Where are they located and why?*

It was through asking questions like these when I was writing copy for the launch of a

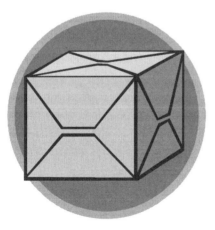

range of organic bread that I discovered that each loaf took four days to make from start to finish. This fact formed part of the headline and helped establish the loaves as a truly different, delicious product worthy of a premium price tag.

Use the product

Above all, take every chance you can to use the products in real life. If it's bath oil, take a soak. If it's food, get munching. If clothing, try the garments on. (I have been known to squeeze an arm into a tiny child's jacket before now, just to try and get an idea of what it might feel like.) Scotts & Co find that one of the best ways is to take products home and use them not just once but for a week or so. "It really helps us find the added-value elements that might otherwise get missed" said Group Buying Director, Victoria Laws.

Features and benefits

The aim of the interrogation is to explore every feature of the product and start to understand the benefits to the customer. It's the benefits that sell, not the features and your headline needs to be based around your biggest benefit. As Lord Beaverbrook said, "Always put your biggest strawberry on top of the basket."

Finding the benefit

A feature is what the product does and a benefit is what the product does for your customer, as in these examples:

FEATURE	BENEFIT
A loan	*The holiday of a lifetime or the car of your dreams*
Raincoats for children	*Longer playtimes, happy children*
Doormats that actively trap dirt	*Cleaner floors for longer*
Contains jojoba oil	*Softer skin*
Carbonated soft drink of vegetable extract	*Refreshment*

The difference between features and benefits is one of the hardest concepts to get to grips with. It sounds simple, and when you get it right it's perfectly obvious in hindsight, yet time and again people struggle to find the benefit of their own products.

If you're having trouble finding the benefit of a particular feature, here's a tip. Picture your customer in your mind. You tell them the feature and they look suitably unimpressed. With a slight sneer, they say to you, "So what?" How do you answer them? Whatever you say is your benefit. You then just need to work out the best way to communicate that in the copy.

On websites, it's generally best to play it safe and describe the benefit simply, such as "Genuine Turtle Mat 'dirt-trapper' mats give you clean floors for longer." This headline gets the message over and includes two keywords 'dirt-trapper' and 'clean floors'. In print, however, you can be more creative, with attention-grabbing headlines such as "Life's too short to mop floors". Search engine spiders don't understand it, but customers do, and it makes them smile, read on and buy.

Structuring your copy

Armed with these two pieces of knowledge, you're now set to start writing. This is where it's helpful to have a structure or framework around which you can build your copy. Selling is a sequential process so first you must grab the reader's attention. Then get them a little bit interested. Next lead them to really, really want the product. Only then do you ask for the sale. These steps are known as AIDA, which stands for

Attention
Interest
Desire & Action

It is a mirror of the way all consumers buy any product. Whether they're purchasing something inconsequential, like a chocolate bar, or major, like a car, the process always follows this same logical series of steps. First a thought appears in the person's mind, and they look around to see where can get the item. If it's a Mars Bar they might simply walk past a kiosk and see sweets for sale. If it's a car they may start browsing brochures, looking online or going to showrooms. Then they weigh up the options and consider which one they like best. Finally they come to a decision and hand over the money.

The time it takes for the customer to go through all these stages can vary considerably, from just moments for confectionery to weeks or months for the car. However, the stages that they go through are always the same and in the same order.

Standard framework for copy

AIDA is not a new idea, as the acronym was first coined in 1898 by an American businessman called Elias St Elmo Leonard. You'll find it in almost any textbook on marketing and copywriting, as it has become the standard framework for all advertising copy from sales letters and advertisements to individual pieces of product copy, both online and offline.

It's not just for the words either. The visuals of a classic catalogue page also follow the hierarchy of buying. Typically the layout starts with a headline and large photograph to attract attention, then sub-heads and product copy to convert interest into desire, and finally detailed specification, pricing and the web address and orderline so that the customer can buy the goods.

To illustrate the way AIDA works in almost any sales situation, here's an example of a man in a pub trying to persuade you to buy a TV.

ATTENTION /
AWARENESS

The consumer becomes aware that items are for sale that they may be interested in. At this stage they are not looking to buy, they just want to find out more.

THE BEGINNING
A statement of superiority or the single best reason to buy the product. It can also be an offer or simply, as in this case, making you aware.

INTEREST

The consumer has a notion that these are products that might interest them, and their attention is engaged. At this stage they are open to finding out more but are still not ready to buy.

THE MIDDLE
Expands on the key benefit, introduces new features or attributes of the product or service and their benefits.

Whilst 'Attention' and 'Action' are often very distinct behavioural steps, the moment when 'Interest' slips into 'Desire' can be quite subtle and indistinct.

DESIRE /
DECISION

This is the tipping point where the con-sumer moves from having a passive interest to actively wanting the product. They have decided to purchase and made their choice.

Our dodgy sales-man might change what he says depending on who he's talking to.

ACTION

He's persuaded you to buy, and now he's telling you exactly what you have to do next.

THE END
Clear instruc-tions on how to buy (or any other intended action. On a website, this could be to sign up for a newsletter, for example).

AIDA

Attention or Awareness

One way to get attention is with a great photograph and a benefit led headline. At one time it was known as the USP or 'Unique Selling Proposition' but that concept has fallen out of fashion because virtually no products are unique these days. (And anything which is truly unique can be copied very quickly.)

Awareness can be enough if you're selling something the customer knows they want, such as a replacement vacuum cleaner bag. Attention is more important when the product is something they're not likely to know about, such as an innovative new type of vacuum cleaner.

Interest and desire (or decision)

These are not two separate steps, but more a gradual progression from passive interest to active desire. (Desire, in this context, means the customer has made up their mind and reached the decision to buy.)

The key to getting them to this point is to write about the benefits. How will it make them feel good? What problem will it solve? How will it improve their lives? Of course, it may be necessary to mention the features, but always explain why they're a good thing.

Say, for example, you're writing about a cycling glove. It might be obvious from the photograph that it has a mesh back, not that it has an anti-slip palm. You need to tell them that the palm feels tacky and go on to explain that it gives great control of the bike. It's also worth mentioning that the mesh keeps their hands cool. Don't hope they will work out the connection themselves, as they probably won't.

Action

At this point your customer has decided that they want your product or service. They are now receptive to and eager for information about colours, sizes and prices.

However, that is not enough to guarantee the sale. To get the customer to act you must also tell them very clearly what they should do next. People love shopping and enjoy having new things. It's thrilling and uplifting, so don't shy away from asking for the sale (or whatever other action you want your reader to take).

Variations of AIDA

Over the years, the AIDA formula has been adapted or added to. One version is called AIDAS with the S standing for 'Subsequent Sales', which emphasises the importance of building repeat business.

Another is AIDCA in which the C stands for 'Credibility' or 'Conviction'. This is a little misleading, as it is not a stage in itself but something which runs through all the stages like veins in blue cheese. Credibility means that the customer is convinced you are trustworthy, and that you will deliver the product that you promise. This is achieved through the cumulative effect of a number of elements such as visual devices like guarantees, padlock symbols on your website, good design, branding, and a tone of voice that sounds sincere and has 'verisimilitude' or the appearance of truth.

Remember, though, that AIDA is a useful tool not a hard and fast rule. The framework will be applied differently depending on factors such as the product, the target audience, the offer, the media and the creative presentation. It is an art, not a science, and you need to use judgement, knowledge of your customer and your product, and a healthy dose of common sense.

AIDA in action - example

The AIDA formula can be applied to almost any piece of copy. Here's an example on some packaging, which is short but follows the framework perfectly.

"This is old fashioned, tasty biltong just like you see hanging in local butcher's shops in South Africa. When I left the country, I really missed it. Taking the best cuts of well-hung meat from our own herds of buffalo and cattle we tried and tested many recipes to create the biltong I had dreamt about.

Made the authentic way by marinating and drying the meat, our organic beef biltong has a traditional flavour while our buffalo biltong is naturally lower in fat and has a rich, earthy flavour. Both can be further enhanced by enjoying with our organic ale and lager."

Jody Scheckter
Founder, Laverstoke Park Farm

A	*This is old fashioned, tasty biltong just like you see hanging in local butcher's shops in South Africa.*	*Best benefit first – taste.*
I	*When I left the country, I really missed it. Taking the best cuts of well-hung meat from our own herds of buffalo and cattle we tried and tested many recipes to create the biltong I had dreamt about.*	*The benefit is expanded and further benefits of authenticity and quality are introduced. The story-telling quality and the fact that this is 'the biltong I had dreamt about' adds emotional benefits.*
D	*Made the authentic way by marinating and drying the meat, our organic beef biltong has a traditional flavour while our buffalo biltong is naturally lower in fat and has a rich, earthy flavour.*	*The copy now goes into more detailed information about how the product is made, with information to support the opening benefits*
A	*Both can be further enhanced by enjoying with our organic ale and lager.*	*The copy encourages action by promising enjoyment. It also introduces a cross-sell.*
C	*Jody Scheckter Founder Laverstoke Park Farm*	*Credibility comes from a variety of sources. The tone of voice is authentic and personal. Visual clues in the packaging include Jody Scheckter's signature, pictures of cows and buffalo, a guarantee statement, awards for the product and the address of the farm.*

Tone of voice

The final thing you need to bear in mind when writing copy is tone of voice. There are two aspects to this. Firstly your copy will be more powerful and effective if you have an active rather than a passive tone of voice. Secondly, your choice of words and sentence structure should reflect your brand personality and be appropriate for your target audience.

Active tone of voice

Always assume the sale when writing copy and write in the present tense whenever possible. You can always spot amateur copy as it uses the word 'will' – as in

'This limited edition bowl will look superb in any room.'

When the word 'will' is deleted, the sentence becomes much more vivid

'This limited edition bowl looks superb in any room.'

It's no longer a vague future promise but a present reality. Here are some more ideas:

Replace passive phrases like these...	.. with active phrases like these
If you order...	*When you order...*
Customers can buy...	*You can buy...*
We will send you...	*You will receive...*
Simply by picking up the phone you could have...	*Phone now for...*
We'd be happy to help	*We're always happy to help*
You will be guaranteed	*You are guaranteed*
Learn Spanish in no time with this DVD	*The DVD that has you speaking Spanish in no time*
If you don't love this ice cream we'll refund your money	*You'll love this ice cream or your money back*
All credit card transactions are automatically processed over our state of the art server	*Your credit card details are fully protected by our state of the art server*

Replace long Latin words like these...	...with short, punchy, Saxon words like these
LONG	**SHORT**
Receive ▶	*Get*
Complimentary ▶	*Free*
Utilised ▶	*Use*
Purchase ▶	*Buy*
Expectation ▶	*Hope*
At this moment in time ▶	*Now*

Cut out negative or depressing words like these...	Instead use positive, uplifting words like these...
NEGATIVE	**POSITIVE**
Don't	*FREE*
Not	*NEW*
Hard	*EASY/SIMPLE*
Difficult	*LOVE*
Form (as in Order Form)	*TRUST*
Fee	*HAPPY*
Decision	*SAFE*
But	*IMPORTANT*
Try	*PROOF*
Should	*YES*
Commit	*YOU*
Depress	*MAGIC*
	HURRY
	BARGAIN

Brand personality

Your tone of voice is your corporate identity in words. Personality comes through in the vocabulary and to a lesser extent, the sentence structure. Compared with product and customer knowledge, the tone of voice is relatively superficial. If AIDA is the framework, the tone of voice is rather like choosing the final paint colour. It takes surprisingly few words to create an entirely different mood.

Below are three sentences all describing clothes but each one is designed to appeal to a very different target audience; young trendy guys, fashion conscious younger women and sophisticated older ladies. It should be easy to spot which is which, even though there's only half a dozen words or so for each one.

- *Silky-soft cashmere inspired by the catwalks of Milan*
- *Sharp threads for straight talkers*
- *Deliciously cute tops in yummy candy colours*

If you're writing the copy yourself then here's a tip. Don't worry too much about tone of voice in your first draft. Keep thinking about the person you're writing to and much of the right tone of voice will come naturally. It's more important to get the benefits across and the AIDA structure right. You can always weave in a few expressive words at the editing stage.

Writing to length

Nearly all copy has to be written to a particular format, and writing to length is part of the skill of copywriting. In the world of ink, paper and postage costs, every square inch costs money so catalogue copy, advertisements and leaflets often have a tight word count.

It's tempting to think that web copy can be as long or as short as you like, because the pages can 'stretch' if more room is needed. However, sometimes web copy is even more restrictive than print. Some CMS (Content Management Systems) limit the character count of certain parts of the site. Web developers and SEO consultants often have strict specifications for word length of different types of copy.

Each website is different, but it's common for headings to be limited to around 65 characters and descriptions to 150 characters. Depending on the way the site is built there may be a requirement for all copy to follow a particular format, such as a headline and some bullet points, followed by 3-4 short paragraphs, each with a heading, and usually about 150-200 words.

That means you have to get the message across in as few words as possible, and fewer words are always harder to write. As George Bernard Shaw once wrote "I'm sorry this letter is so long, I didn't have time to make it shorter." Whether the copy is online or offline, always make sure you are aware of the word length at the start of the brief, to save expensive re-writes and hassle later on.

Writing online copy

These basic principles of copywriting hold true for online and offline copy, but web copy has one extra factor; SEO or Search Engine Optimisation. The better your SEO, the more likely you are to appear at the top of the page – for free. However, SEO is a complex and ever changing subject, so this section simply aims to cover some of the general principles, and I am grateful for the expert help and contributions of Shahid Awan, Global SEO Director for www.hotels.com and owner of www.wristwatches.co.uk.

How search engines work

Google and other search engines decide your ranking by sending 'spiders' to 'crawl' your website and index it, one piece of data at a time. This information is then subjected to a complex automated analysis using mathematical algorithms.

Hundreds of criteria are evaluated, although what they all are and the weight given to each one is a closely guarded secret. However, we do know that Google, and other search engines, look for two things when ranking your site: Relevance and Authority.

The reason they do this is so that when someone uses Google the results that come up provide a solution to his or her problem or desires. If the sites suggested match the searcher's needs accurately, they are more likely to use Google again next time, thus maintaining their position as the number one search engine.

Authority

Authority comes largely from how other people regard you, in particular when other sites think so highly of your site that they link theirs to yours.

One of the most effective ways to improve your search engine rankings is to have lots of external links pointing to the most relevant landing page on your website. Quality counts more than quantity so a link from a major national newspaper or a government-owned site could have far more impact on your SEO than a dozen mentions by small time bloggers.

It's also important that the anchor text (visible, clickable hypertext links) on the external website incorporates keywords that are relevant to the page they point to. If it simply says 'click here', you get no benefit at all. This is an example of a well-phrased link which would appear on the external website. (Mens' appears without an apostrophe as that's how most people search).

Find a big selection of **mens watches** *at* **wristwatches.co.uk**

Here we can see that the keyword is **mens watches** and it would link to a specific mens watches page at ***http://www.wristwatches.co.uk/mens-watches.htm***

The implication for your web copy is that in order to persuade influential sites to link to your site, the content on your site must offer something of value or interest.

Relevance

Keywords play a big role in relevance as defined by Google. A keyword is simply a word or words used by an internet user when they type into a search engine. (It's always called a 'keyword' even if a whole phrase is used). Weight is given to

 ♦ *the specific keywords that are used in the copy*

 ♦ *how often keywords are used*

 ♦ *where they appear (eg: in headings and bullet points, earlier or later in the text)*

 ♦ *how frequently it is refreshed and updated – the more often the better as far as Google is concerned*

However, the overall quality of the copy is also important as Google wants to give its users a good experience by showing them good, useful sites. It's not enough to simply string a load of keywords together.

Creating customer-friendly keyword-rich copy

From a copywriting perspective, the first thing to keep in mind about keywords is that they are simply the words **an internet user** uses to search. When they're looking for something (either to buy or to find out more) it's what they key into the search box at the top of the screen.

I've highlighted the words internet user (above) because it's worth spending a moment to reflect what that means... a person. In other words; we are back to the heart of all marketing and copywriting – people.

What this means is that if you understand your customers to the point where you can 'put yourself in their skin and walk around' as the proverb goes, you're half way towards writing search engine optimised copy naturally.

Google and other search engines give higher ranking to well-written or customer-focused copy, which is a great help as this is also the sort of copy that's more likely to persuade people to buy once they reach your site.

Here are five steps towards achieving that. The first three are to do with keyword research, part of the briefing process, and the last two are relevant if you are the actual person writing the copy.

1 Get together a seed list of keywords

2 Research your keywords to find out which ones are widely used

3 Put your list of keywords in order with the best at the top

4 Put your list away and write your copy

5 Go back the next day and weave in the keywords

Let's look in a bit more detail at each of those five steps.

1 Create a seed list of keywords

If you're starting from scratch, the first place to look is your product specification which might include the product description (eg: bedside cabinet), generic description (eg: mahogany furniture) and general categories (eg: bedroom furniture). Your web developer, SEO consultant and analytics expert may have a view, so do ask them. Finally use a big dose of common sense. Put yourself into the mind of the consumer. If you were looking for products like these, what would you key into Google to try and find them? Jot them down.

Also add in synonyms, and if you're scratching your head because the last time you heard the word 'synonym' was when you were wearing a school uniform, then it means two words that are spelled differently that mean the same (such as 'present' and 'gift').

If you're updating an existing site, then take a look at the 'entrance keywords' report of your web analytics and build on that list. Shahid recommends this as a quarterly exercise to make sure your copy stays ahead of the competition.

2 *Research your keyword seed list*

This is dead easy to do. Just log onto Google's free keyword tool **https://adwords. Google.com/select/KeywordToolExternal**, type your keywords in and up it pops with a huge long list of similar words. Next to them, rather handily, in a nice, neat and easy to read column is a number which is 'volumes of search'. The ones with big numbers next to them are the ones you want to concentrate on. The bigger the number, the more likely it is that people will type in that word or phrase.

This nifty tool will also come up with suggestions for keywords (eg: if you key in 'gifts' it will also show you the volumes for 'gift', 'presents' and 'Christmas gifts' and many more). Typically there will be a handful of search terms that number in the millions, a few six figures, and the rest much lower. Because the columns are neatly laid out it's very easy to spot the high volumes. Just give them a quick swish with a highlighter pen and there's your list.

Why is Google so kind and helpful as to provide this useful free service? It's because they make a lot of their money from a form of advertising called Adwords (or Pay Per Click) and the keyword tool encourages advertisers to invest in it.

There are also some paid-for research tools such as **www.wordtracker.com** and **www.keyworddiscovery.com** although there might well be more by the time you read this. These services give you a higher level of sophistication to help pick out keywords, especially 'latent' keywords which don't seem to bear any relation to your product, but are nonetheless used by customers to search for it. These can be real diamonds, as your competitors probably aren't using them, so they'll cost less to buy and could be much more effective.

These paid-for tools are easier and faster to use than Google's free tool and give you more keywords. They also analyse the keywords to highlight which ones are most effective and which have serious competition.

One thing to look out for is plurals. Very often the plural or singular of the same keyword will have hugely different search volumes. When I first heard this I was baffled. Why do people key in 'digital camera' four times more often than 'digital cameras'?

It made no sense until I found myself searching for an outfit for my daughter's first holy communion. I noticed that I'd typed 'holy communion dress' into the search box. I wondered why I had done that, especially when I was expecting to see a number of outfits, not just a lone frock.

Then I realized it's because I was looking for a 'dress' whereas the company is selling 'dresses'. The customer is always interested in only one thing – themselves.

3 Put your keywords in order

This is simple. You've got your list, highlighted the big players – just put them in order of popularity. Job done.

4 Hide your keyword list while you write

This may sound a surprising thing to suggest – after all you've just expended time and energy putting your perfect keyword list together. Why should you temporarily forget all about it?

The reason is that when you're writing your copy, it's vital to have a real connection with your customer. After all, search engine spiders don't have wallets, they don't own credit cards, and they have no desire to buy from you. People buy, and people need scintillating copy, not a bundle of keywords

That's why it's so much better to free up your mind so that you're just thinking about your customer and your product. Once you've written your first draft there's plenty of time to add keywords in later.

You may find a lot of the keywords already in your copy. Has anyone ever said to you, "Don't think of a pink elephant"? It's impossible not to. In the same way, the very action of reading the keywords means they will probably seep into your writing without any effort.

5 Edit in the keywords afterwards

The next day, go back and look at your draft with the keyword list to hand. A simple re-write, a bit of light editing, and some chopping and changing of sentences to weave in more keywords will improve the chances of it being found by potential customers. Try to put the best keywords at the start or in bullets and headings as these are the ones the search engines give more weight to.

How to edit in keywords

Aim to squeeze in the extra keywords in a fairly natural way. Here's a sentence for some mugs:

"Perfect for lovers of nature, these high quality mugs feature finely detailed drawings of jungle animals".

This could be very slightly amended to read:

"A great gift for nature lovers. Porcelain mugs featuring finely detailed drawings of rainforest animals."

The sense and the word length is much the same, but the second version includes the keywords 'gift' and 'porcelain mugs'. The term 'rainforest animals' is searched five times more frequently than 'jungle animals'.

Avoid keyword stuffing

However, take care to keep it sounding natural and don't jam in too many keywords, as this becomes 'keyword stuffing' which can get you downgraded or blacklisted. How do you know what is too many? One guide is a useful free tool called **www.spidertest.com.** Just type in your web page and it evaluates whether you've got too many or too few keywords.

An even easier way to tell is to use common sense – just read it. If the copy is gibberish, makes you cringe or feel bored you've probably got too many keywords. Not only will it fail to interest humans, it probably won't score very highly with search engine spiders either.

Remember too that your copy is only one small part of your total SEO strategy. Many other factors play a part, so it makes sense to write for your customers, rather than trying to force in too many keywords. There is no point in getting lots of people coming to your site if you can't persuade them to buy when they get there.

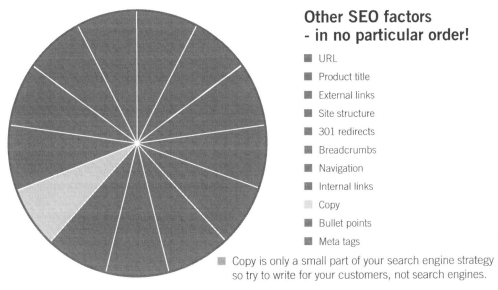

Other SEO factors
- in no particular order!

- URL
- Product title
- External links
- Site structure
- 301 redirects
- Breadcrumbs
- Navigation
- Internal links
- Copy
- Bullet points
- Meta tags

Copy is only a small part of your search engine strategy so try to write for your customers, not search engines.

The rules of SEO are constantly changing. Google and other search engines regularly change their algorithms and competition also plays a part. It's much easier to get to the number one position on the page when competition is low, but as it increases, you need to take action to keep ahead of the game. So what's the best way to stay ahead? Shahid advises, "If you can't complete a page 100% just do the best you can – let's say 60% of page copy. Take a view to go back and update the page frequently. The more a page is updated, the more likely a search engine will come back and spider it. Think fresh and frequently updated content".

You can also turn to Google's own website for advice – it's a wonderful source of clear, jargon-free information. Google itself suggests that the best way to get continually high search engine rankings is to "Provide high-quality content on your pages. This is the single most important thing to do." Luckily, that's also what human beings want too, so everyone wins.

Summary

To write effective copy, you need to know your product inside out and your customer as if they're a good friend.

Structure your copy in a hierarchy that mirrors how people buy, using the tried and tested AIDA framework – Attention, Interest, Desire, Action.

Tell people what your product will do for them, by focusing on benefits rather than features.

Always put your best benefit first. On websites, the rule is 'clear not clever' but in print you can be more creative.

Always write for one person as if you were speaking to them face to face.

This applies to all copy, both online and offline. Online copy needs to be written slightly differently to incorporate elements such as keywords which will help increase natural search engine rankings.

6 | **Principles of copywriting**

7 | Web copy and other online media

A website is a hungry beast when it comes to written content. To keep it in peak condition your site needs regular feeding with a varied diet of many different types of copy. Some of this will be user-generated content (known as UGC) – things like forums and reviews – but the vast bulk will be copy you generate yourself.

Whether you generate this content by briefing it out or writing it yourself, it helps to be very clear-headed about the purpose of each of these types of content. Why? The copy will be easier to write and easier to evaluate. It also helps to smooth the approvals process. If everyone on your team is in agreement on the objectives, they're more likely to agree on the copy – well, that's the theory anyway.

Another reason for getting clarity on the characteristics of different types of web content is to help match the right sort of writer to each type of copy. Product copy may need to be written by someone with a classical copywriting background who knows how to sell, whereas a 'Hot Topics' blog is best done by a journalist with constant access to insider information so that the posts are genuinely fresh and insightful.

Web copy has to be clear, not clever

One thing that all web content has in common is that it must be very, very straightforward. That's because search engines simply don't understand clever headlines, puns and plays on words. Web copy has to be clear, not clever.

On websites, every page counts, because search engines don't look at websites as a whole, they look at individual web pages. Typically a retail website needs high quality written content for:

- *URLs, titles and tags*
- *Link copy*
- *Home page*
- *Landing page*
- *Category and sub-category reviews*
- *Product copy*
- *Static copy such as*
  - *Frequently asked questions*
  - *Delivery*
  - *Location/contact us*
  - *Small print, such as the privacy policy and legal notices*
  - *Information such as environmental policies and access policies.*
- *Advice copy such as*
  - *Buyers guides*
- *Checkout*

URL, Titles and Tags

In SEO terms, your URL, Title, Title Tag and Meta Descriptions are some of the most important parts of your site, so it's worth taking the time to write them well. But they're not just useful to get your site ranked higher by Google. They are also helpful for your reader so that they can see where they are in the site at a glance.

The URL of each page on your site is given a lot of weight by Google so a well-written one can give your SEO a real boost. It should describe the content in real words, not numbers or symbols like %£"cc=CGY%&hl=_%""en&)rlz=&o0mh*=. Another good reason to avoid long, meaningless URLs is that tests show that people are more inclined to click on a short URL than a long one.

The title tag and the meta descriptions could well be what's displayed to your potential customer in the results page that shows on screen after they've done a search. Your site is there because Google has decided that your site is one of the ones that's most relevant to that person's search. It's being presented to a potential customer – one that's already shown an interest in you by the nature of the search that led to your site coming up. Keep that in mind. You are not writing a technical blurb, but an ad headline that might persuade a hot lead to click through to your site.

Title tag copy

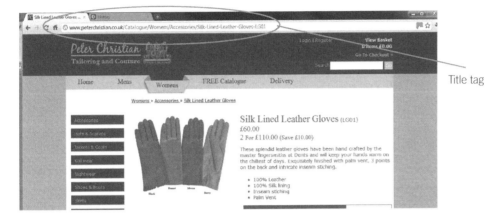

Title tag

The title tag is usually 68 characters or less and appears in the title box at the top of the screen, with the primary keyword in the first part of the copy. The keyword will probably contain a generic description of your product. If the product is a well known brand name, this can also go in the title tag. You can also put a secondary keyword in the title, so a title tag for children's arm bands might read: 'Swim floats. (Brand name) armbands for kids'.

Description tag copy

The description tag is usually 170 words or less and should also contain the primary keyword. It supports and extends the title. It's ideal to write this in sentences as this makes it more likely that Google will show this text in the search results.

There are no guarantees of this – Google could choose to put up a snippet from any part of your web page – but tests show that when the description is well-written, it's more likely to be shown. Plus, the description tag is not just for search engines, it's also for humans, and people respond better to well-written sentences rather than a string of keywords.

In the description tag, keep the focus on the primary and secondary keywords. Bringing in other keywords can dilute down the message, and make it appear less 'relevant' in Google's eyes, which means you'll get put lower down the page.

Internal link copy

Another effective way to improve your search engine rankings is to include internal 'anchor texts' – visible, clickable hypertext links on your site. Search engines give weight to the page that the link is pointing to (not the page the link is on) and like the all-important external links, these internal links need to incorporate relevant keywords in order to benefit your SEO. They should be considered as copy and crafted as carefully as an advertising headline.

Some ways to incorporate keywords into these internal links are:

a) *Cross sell:*

Eg: On a page selling torches, the link could say: "Remember to buy two **AA batteries**" or "Do you need **AA batteries** with that?"

b) *Upsell*

Eg: "These are standard AA batteries. We also sell longer-lasting **Alkaline AA batteries**"

c) *Recommendations*

Eg: You might also like our "**head torches**"

d) *Go back to the top of the page*

A neat trick is to simply add to the bottom of every page on your site a line saying "**Go back to the top of the AA batteries page**"

e) *Cheap tricks*

One of the most searched terms on the web is 'Cheap' as in 'Cheap holidays', 'Cheap beds' and so on. However, the last thing customers want is anything cheap and nasty. What they really mean when they type in cheap is 'top quality at a cheap price'.

It's a dilemma, as few websites want to be seen offering 'cheap' goods. However, as it's such a high-ranking search term one way to do it is to use internal links at the bottom of the page, saying "We don't sell **cheap phones** but we do sell top quality brands at great value prices." The link could go to either a page of clearance items, or to an article about what to look for in a good phone and why a cheap phone isn't good value for money.

These principles also apply to external links, one of the most important elements of SEO. If you can persuade other sites to link to yours, always try to make sure that the hypertext link on their site is written in such a way that it includes relevant keywords as in the examples above. A link that just says 'click here' is of no value to you at all.

Home page copy

The main role of the copy on your home page is to say "This is what we do – and this is what's in it for you". You have just moments to let them know who you are and why they should stay on the site. The copy needs to include a simple statement or value proposition that tells them at a glance – from the customer's point of view, not the company's. Additional copy should expand on this and incorporate keywords that apply to the whole site.

Of course, there are lots of other functions of the home page. It's for navigation, it's to draw your customers in, stop them leaving, get them to sign up to a newsletter, show them your bestsellers, reassure them, get them in the mood to buy, keep their basket in view and more.

But these are essentially functions of the architecture of the site, rather than the opening welcome message. It's amazing how many websites simply don't make it clear what they're offering, which is a pity, because it's one of the reasons people leave the site – fast. Keep your messages simple. "Hand made gifts for busy mums" is much better than "Welcome to our website where you'll find a wonderful range of hand made gifts to suit every budget. We believe that mums are heroes, so our range is carefully selected to appeal to the fabulous mothers of the world".

Landing page copy

Technically any page of your website can be a landing page, but here I mean a page that you have created specially for people to land on when they have clicked on an Adword or email or typed in a specific URL that they may have seen in a promotion.

When this happens, acknowledge the route they took to get to you, with a similar visual look and copy such as "Thank you for clicking through from the email we sent you" or "Here's the special offer on duffle coats that we promised you".

Category overviews and sub-category overviews

This is the copy that pops up when you click on a category heading, usually found on one of the drop down menus on the main navigation.

In this example for the clothes company Peter Christian the main category is 'Mens' and the sub-categories – trousers, socks, nightshirts and so on – are on the drop down menu.

The main aims for this type of copy are to:

a) *Tell your customers what they can expect to find there.*

b) *Curry favour with search engine spiders by feeding them relevant keywords.*

c) *Reinforce your brand message.*

In other words, the category copy is a signpost to help your customers find their way around. It's also part of your organic search engine optimisation.

When writing or reviewing this kind of copy bear in mind that you are simply telling your customers what they will find, not trying to sell the products. This is not the place to try and sell the product – your job here is to get them to click through to the next page.

Category overviews can be surprisingly hard to write well. There's a sense that it's only necessary for search engine purposes. After all, if the customer has clicked on 'citrus fruits' they know what they're likely to find there without needing a tedious message along the lines of "We have a massive range of citrus fruits. Grapefruits, oranges, lemons, limes we have citrus fruits galore".

The other issue is that they can end up sounding like a list "You'll find this, and that, and we also sell the other". However, there are a few tricks you can use to avoid this. Break up the sentences so that you mention just two or three items together, and look for products that start with the same letter so that you can use alliteration. "Looking for a big, juicy selection of citrus fruits? We have some of the choicest grapefruits and oranges on the web, and our lemons and limes are pretty sharp too."

Avoid starting your category overviews with "Welcome to the Widgets section of our website". Instead try to draw the reader in by starting with a verb or choosing phrases appropriate to the category you're describing, as in these opening lines to category overviews for **http://uk.shop.com**:

Raise a glass to our fantastic selection of bar accessories.

Make light work of choosing a new lampshade.

Find your way to a great deal on sat navs.

Like the sound of great prices on audio?

Have you heard about our fantastic selection of speakers?

There's pots of choice here in the cookware section.

An often overlooked use of category overviews is to help reinforce your brand. You can weave in messages about what you stand for and why it's worth buying from your site:

"When you buy from the world's no 1 citrus fruit store, you're guaranteed that every segment is deliciously juicy."

Far from being a sop to the search engines, the best category overviews are genuinely helpful. They can give the user a sense of the breadth of the range, a flavour of the products on offer, and convince the customer it's worth their while drilling on down.

Web product copy

When you're writing about an individual product, the 'formula' or framework is the same as for catalogue copy or indeed any written piece of sales material. You begin with a key benefit or statement of superiority, describe the benefits and end on a call to action. See page 87 for more explanation of this 'formula' known as AIDA (which stands for Attention, Interest, Desire and Action).

The main differences between web product copy and catalogue product copy are:

a) Copy for the web can be longer, provided it is written and laid out in a way that it can be 'skimmed' quickly and easily. In fact it is often a requirement to have longer copy to bolster your natural search engine rankings. However, do check that the individual product pages on a website can 'stretch' as some sites have restrictive CMS (or Content Management Systems) which means that certain sections have a maximum word count or character count.

   Websites often have a specific format (often decided by the web developers) including bullet points and paragraphs with headings. In computer code terms, the different headings are known as H1, H2 and so on down to H6. They may be limited to a certain number of characters, so always check before writing.

   These, as well as the bullet points and any highlighted words are given more weight by search engines. This is where the most important keywords should go, with the primary keyword in H1 (the main headline) and secondary keywords in H2, H3 and so on (the sub-headings).

   This type of format is not just spider-friendly but consumer-friendly as well. If someone is in a hurry, they can get the topline information fast, while those with more time (and interest) can read the full story.

b) Web product copy usually needs to be rich in keywords. The essence here is 'rich' not 'stuffed'. The copy should flow and be a good read with the keywords as a natural part of the core message.

   However, there is another key difference and that is in the call to action. On the web, it's not enough to simply ask for the sale, we have to soothe and reassure our potential buyers that they're doing the right thing.

The psychology of web shopping

I find it fascinating that despite our being in the high-tech 21st century, human beings still react in an 'old-brain' way to the internet – especially just at the moment we're about to buy. The act of pressing the button to complete the purchase induces a complex biological reaction that causes huge anxiety – the old 'fight or flight' reflex of caveman days.

This was observed during the sophisticated usability studies carried out by US firm Eight by Eight. Participants are wired up to heart rate monitors and brain scanners. Scientists take saliva swabs to measure hormone changes and there is even a former FBI body language expert closely observing to see what's happening.

Eight by Eight noticed that when people are about to pay, their feet start twitching and tensing under the table. Graphs show an increase in heart rate and a massive rush of adrenaline.

When I first heard this, I found it hard to believe. Why should the body react so strongly to a harmless computer in the comfort of your own home? However the next time I was making an internet purchase I tried to observe myself dispassionately – and what I discovered was extraordinary. I felt the anxiety, I was aware of my heart beating faster, my toes scrunched up a little under the table and I had a sort of heightened sense of being. It was so strong, I was amazed I'd never noticed before – and it was exactly as the research had suggested.

What can happen next is that the customer decides to look at another site, does another search to see if they can get it cheaper, or gets cold feet and changes their mind altogether.

Calls to action in web product copy

The implications of this for the product copy are that the final paragraph should give lots of reassurance to potential customers. The kind of messages that make customers feel safe, or push them to making the decision to buy right now are:

- *This is the only place where they can buy such an item (so it's not worth going elsewhere).*

- *You have a price promise (so they can't get it cheaper anywhere else).*

- *It's covered by a full money back guarantee (so there's no problem if it goes wrong).*

- *Stock is going fast (so they could miss out).*

- *Lots of other people have bought it. (This simple reassurance is incredibly effective on the web. Simply knowing that other people have trodden the same path and done the same things is a huge motivator.)*

Section (or Static) copy

This is all the copy that you have to have on a website that isn't actually product copy. It's sometimes known as static copy, as it's part of the structure of the site rather than products which are constantly being removed, changed or added.

These are some of the most read pages on the site so it is worthwhile investing time and effort to get them right. All too often the static copy is created in-house by someone in the operations department. It is written from the company's point of view rather than the customer's with off-putting instructions and caveats like: "Customers must fill in… Failure to do so… It is your responsibility to make sure that …" Negative messages like this can destroy the sale so take care to word these important parts of the site in a way that reinforces your brand and encourages customers to buy.

These are some of the main kinds of section copy:

♦ *FAQs*

♦ *Buyer's guides*

♦ *Checkout*

♦ *Legal notices*

♦ *Location and Contact Us*

♦ *Environmental policy*

Delivery and returns

Most websites now have a link on the home page and information about delivery on every product page. That's good news as it means your customers don't have to slog all the way to the end of the checkout process to find out how much you're going to charge them to get the goods to their door. A good number of those potential customers simply won't bother – they'll just leave the site, and that's just potential profits flying out of the window. In fact, issues around delivery charges are one of the biggest causes of 'abandoned baskets'.

Conversely, if you offer free delivery (even if it's only above a certain spend) then it's a real shame not to let people know about it.

If your delivery section is a mass of text all in the same font size, try doing this exercise. Print it off and take three highlighter pens. Use one for all the positives (eg: they have a generous 21 days to change their mind, returns are free), another colour for any negatives (eg: it has to be unused and in original packaging) and third for information that only a tiny percentage of your customers need to know (such as delivery to the Highlands and Islands).

Look at your positives and make those the key focus of your message, and put them in sub-headings. Where you have a negative, try to word it in a neutral way. The final colour is information that can be a simple link to another page or a tab on the same page (for delivery to all other destinations, click here).

That way you should end up with a nice clean and easy to read page. Customers can quickly find the information they need, and it creates a good positive impression.

Frequently Asked Questions (FAQs)

This is often the most read page of any website, so make the most of all the rich opportunities offered by this hardworking and underappreciated section. The first thing to bear in mind about Frequently Asked Questions is that they do not have to be questions your customers actually ask frequently.

FAQs are a great chance to re-state your main offer, build your brand, get customers to trust you and want to buy from you. Think about the things you want your customers to know. Do you want to be seen as an expert? Have you got one of the biggest ranges in your sector? Why should you be their number one choice?

Once you know what you want to communicate, you can start to frame the questions. Try to word them in such a way that the questions themselves draw people in and make them want to read the answer, even if they hadn't thought about it themselves. Word them in a way that presents the company in a positive light even without reading the answer such as "How long have you been Britain's biggest supplier of widgets?" And if you can slip a few keywords into your headings that will also help your natural search.

Do divide your FAQs into different sections as this makes it easier for people to hunt for what they want. Feel free to repeat information that may be in other parts of the website, such as delivery charges and contact details. (It's fine to put in internal links to those pages, but also give people the topline so that they're not forced to click on to another page if they just want the basic information.) An FAQ of "How Can I Contact You" might say something like "Our phones are open 24 hours a day on 01234 567890. Our postal address is 12 Anyroad, Townsville, AB12 3CD. If you would like to contact a specific department, click here for detailed information".

Buyer's guides

Buyer's guides are simple factsheets or informative articles that offer useful advice. They are fantastic for both search engine optimisation and to build a relationship with your customers – especially if you're selling something specialist or unusual such as panama hats or golf balls.

When your customer is at the research stage of the buying cycle this information is highly desirable. More importantly they trust you as the source and remember you later when they reach the stage of wanting to buy.

The more varied the selection of products you sell, the more value you'll get from your buyer's guides. Once your customer has bought one product from you, they'll want to come back and view your buyer's guide for another product in the future.

Aim to present the information plainly and helpfully, adding in pictures and diagrams if they are likely to help. Make sure the information is genuinely useful, impartial and comprehensive. For your own convenience, word it in a way that is 'evergreen' so it won't need updating every year. Use generic information whenever possible rather than focusing on this year's current model – unless you are offering a special time limited download.

You might want to think about a template format for your buyer's guides, as it can make them easier to compile and easier to use. Typical headings include:

- *Where to start (a brief overview)*
- *Key features to look for*
- *Jargon explained*
- *Expert opinion*
- *Reviews and testimonials*
- *Leading brands*
- *Price bands*
- *Aftercare*

Another type of buyer's guides are how-to guides. These are more editorial than the pure product-based category overviews. They are designed to inspire the customer or simply help establish your site as a leading expert. Typical subjects might be 'How to clean suede' for a shoe store, or 'How to plan garden lighting' for a site selling outdoor lighting.

They complement the product guides and a good site has a mix of both. For example, a bathroom store might have 'How to get the New York loft look' to inspire casual browsers, and 'How to build a wet-room' for visitors who are further along the buying process. Both are excellent for natural search engine optimisation.

If you're looking for inspiration for buyer's guides, ask your sales and customer services teams what sort of questions come up regularly. Read the magazines your customers are reading. They're a wonderful source of ideas as well as having the right tone of voice. Take a look what people are saying on the forums on your social media sites.

Another source of ideas for buyer's guides is keyword research such as the free keyword suggestion tools offered by Google Adwords or paid-for tools such as Wordtracker. Last year I helped the online study programme Frankly.com develop some lessons on copywriting, which involved writing keyword-rich copy for a fictional cosmetics company called Jaivi. While researching the keyword 'make-up brushes' we discovered that 'How to clean make-up brushes' is a frequently searched term. When you spot clues like this, you can be sure it will make a popular subject for a buyer's guide. With editorials and how-to guides you can have as many as you like as long as the titles are relevant, well-written and appeal to your customers.

Checkout process

Your checkout process deserves some of your best design and copywriting efforts, because it's so easy to lose people here. The more you can do to pull them in, keep them going and not sneaking away from your site the more sales you'll keep. There are lots of poorly constructed checkout paths, and the reality is that a good number of the customers who start out simply don't make it through.

The role of the copy is to guide and reassure and keep the customer moving at every step of the way. It is crucial that the copy, design and the graphics work hand in hand.

To achieve this, you have to understand what the customer is thinking and feeling while they're buying. This is not about paying lip service to some jargon like 'enhancing the customer experience'. It's about being in tune with your customer, connecting with them and writing to them as if they're your best mate (or your gran, or your brother, whoever matches your target audience the best).

At this stage in the sale, there are two big driving forces going on.

1) Frustration – *how long will it take?*

The whole business of checking out is a real bore. The fun bit was doing the shopping, now it's down to tedious form-filling. They want it to be over with as quickly as possible. They are probably also feeling a loss of control. Up until now they could leave the site at any time. Now if they leave the site, they lose the goods they've invested lots of time in choosing. They are stuck there until you release them with a payment confirmation. This makes them feel fretful and frustrated – a bit like when you are on a railway platform waiting for a train that you know is delayed and no-one tells you when it's going to arrive.

2) Fear – *am I doing the right thing?*

As soon as the customer has to part with their cash, all kinds of doubts creep into their mind that simply weren't there when they were cheerily imagining unwrapping their parcel with their new goodies inside. Will I like it? Can I get it cheaper somewhere else? If I wait will the price come down? Should I have it in blue? Do I need it at all? Am I making a mistake? This is a bit like getting to the cinema and seeing a big queue to buy a ticket and wondering if you should bother going.

Do not underestimate these two feelings. They are real and pretty much universal. You should do everything you can to address them, because you will sell more. The way to help your customers overcome these twin sensations is simple. Spoon-feed them helpful, friendly information. It works like a charm.

The information you need to give your customers relates directly to how they are feeling, so you need to give two types of information:

1) To counter frustration – Allow your customer to feel in control by letting them know exactly where they are in the buying process and how much more time it will take. (This is the equivalent of the guard at the train station telling you that the replacement train will be here in five minutes.)

2) To allay fear – Give your customer lots of reassurance that they are doing the right thing. Make them aware that other people have done the same as them. (This is the equivalent of you overhearing someone in the cinema queue saying that this is the fifth time they've seen this film, it's so brilliant.)

So how do you do this in practice? Here are some of the key ways, and you'll notice that they all depend on a subtle combination of copy, graphic design and site structure.

1) *Don't force new customers to register to buy*

Imagine that you've landed on a site, popped a couple of items in the shopping basket and clicked on the 'check out' button. The next thing you're asked for is to register to begin the checkout. This is the online equivalent of a Russian department store where you have to queue up to get a ticket to go to another cash desk. It all seems a bit heavy handed, and a good number of your potential buyers simply won't bother. Case studies by Applied Web Analytics suggest that a quarter of all users click away from the site the moment they are asked to register.

Far better to take all the details, then later on in the checkout ask new customers if they'd like their details stored for next time. Point out all the benefits, such as how much quicker and easier it will be next time they shop with you. Reassure them that their details will be held safely and securely and not passed on.

2) *Have a clear and prominent 'buying thermometer'*

This tells your customer where they are in the checkout process and how much more they have to do. The number of steps here is critical. Five stages are ideal. Three means that each stage is too long, so you'll lose people, and more than five makes it look complicated so your customer is put off before they even start. Stages one and two should be especially quick so that the customer feels they're getting somewhere.

The 'thermometer' visual needs to be strong, simple and easy to understand at a glance. It could be a series of coloured boxes, a little train going along a track, a line of ticks, or anything else that suggests time passing and levels completed.

Typical five stages might be:

♦ *View Basket (with clear buttons for 'checkout now' and 'continue shopping' so the customer feels comfortable about clicking on and off the page)*

♦ *Delivery information*

♦ *Payment information*

♦ *Review your order*

♦ *Confirmation*

Use copy throughout to help guide the customer through the process, soothing and reassuring all the way. It should be written from the customer's point of view, not just a blunt description of what the company wants. So instead of words like 'Correct postcode must be given' go for something like 'Please make sure we have your correct postcode so we can deliver to you faster'.

The words need to be conversational and appropriate to the brand and the target audience, including the descriptions of the stages. For example, the five stages above could be called:

- *Your goodies*
- *Where shall we send your parcel?*
- *How would you like to pay?*
- *One final check of your order*
- *You're done!*

3) Create online forms that reward the user

Make your copy and form layout work with the buying thermometer to guide the user through the process. Aim to make them feel secure and rewarded, with messages like *"Thanks for your address. Now how would you like to pay?"*

Above all, avoid punishing your user for making mistakes. Ask for answers rather than demanding them. Word error messages in a positive way so instead of flashing up "This field must be completed" use a helpful phrase like "Please add in your dialling code".

The worst thing you can do is force the user to start the form again because of one small error, so design the site in a way that preserves information – don't let it all get wiped with one press of the back button.

4) Make it easy to see what answer goes where

When they get to your form, users know that they've got to give you information like the delivery address and how they have to pay. They look first for the boxes they need to fill in, then they look for the labels that tell them which piece of information goes in each box. Make it easy for them by ensuring that you've put the label for each box close to the box it belongs to.

Eye-tracking research by Caroline Jarrett co-author of 'Forms that work: Designing web forms for usability' shows that users focus most closely on the left-hand end of the boxes. That's why it's best to avoid putting information to the right or below the box: users may miss that altogether.

The label for the box can go in this area

Or in this area to the left   *This area is invisible*

This area here is ambiguous:
users may not see it at all until after they've filled in the box,
or they may associate it with the next box

5) *Have full product information visible at the final point of purchase*

Have you ever been just about to buy something on the internet and just wanted one last look just to make sure? When people are about to press the final button they do have thoughts like "Did I book the evening or the matinee performance? Did I click on the size 12 or the size 14?" If it's not there on screen, chances are they'll hit the back button and may even lose the site completely.

That means that all your efforts getting the customer to this critical moment when they're just about to part with their cash are about to slide back to square one. It's like reaching square 99 on the snakes and ladders board and landing on the giant snake that takes you back to the beginning. Don't take the risk – make sure the full listing of goods can be seen by your user at every step.

6) *Delivery information at point of purchase*

How often have you got to a point in the form where you've been asked whether you'd like 'standard delivery' or 'express delivery' with no indication about the costs or timings of either?

This is bound to make your user fret, get frustrated or just give up on you. Make sure that your delivery charges are clearly visible at all times during the checkout process. It's such a shame to lose your potential customer at this point when you're so close to making the sale.

7) *Relevant testimonials, strategically placed right and left*

For over a century testimonials have been a stock-in-trade in press ads, leaflets, and brochures. They worked brilliantly in print and they're even more powerful on websites. They are the ultimate proof to the lone computer user that other humans have done the same as them.

A good place to put testimonials is in the right hand column to act as a hook for any wandering eyes that are losing interest in the site. The key thing is to pick quotes that support whatever is on the main page rather than choosing them at random.

It's not rocket science – but you'd be amazed at how few websites use their testimonials strategically.

WEB PAGE	TESTIMONIAL TYPE	WHO BY
Home page	*General comments about the company*	*Journalists or celebrities*
Category overviews	*General comments about the huge range, ease of navigation, enjoyable experience*	*Journalists, celebrities or customers*

WEB PAGE	TESTIMONIAL TYPE	WHO BY
Product pages	*Specific comments about the quality of products and speed of delivery*	*Customers or journalists*
Delivery pages	*Specific comments about how fast the products arrived, as well as the quality of the packaging and excellent condition of the goods on arrival*	*Customers*
Order form	*Specific comments about how easy it was to return goods, or how well a complaint was dealt with*	*Customers*

Of all these, the most important is the one by the order form. Don't shy away from putting in a genuine testimonial saying how easy it is to return products. This will not encourage returns – it will simply give people a sense of relief at the point of purchase. You will not be planting seeds of doubt, as the customer is already raising objections in their mind. Without any prompting, they will be thinking "What if I don't like it and it's a hassle to send back?" A reassuring quote helps to knock down these last barriers and increase sales.

■ David Nieper uses testimonials and a guarantee to help reassure customers at the critical moment when they are about to pay.

Legal notices, accessibility and privacy policy

Legal notices are such a turn-off for customers. Of course they have to be on the site, but always try to find out from your lawyers whether the words you are given have to be presented exactly as is. Sometimes, there may be other, more user-friendly ways to put the message across, especially in the realms of accessibility and privacy policies.

Of course I'm not suggesting you should do anything illegal or put yourself in a vulnerable position by wilfully ignoring your lawyers. However legal jargon can be a real sales killer. Find out why it has to be on the site. It's always worth asking if there's any way of toning it down or even removing it altogether.

There's a few ways to deal with the legal stuff: **Rewrite, Preface, Relocate**

Rewrite – Edit and reword so that it sounds more friendly. This is particularly relevant to the small print around data protection. There is no standard wording, so provided your meaning is perfectly clear, you could try something nice and friendly such as "Fancy some freebies? Tick here and we'll ping some news, comps and offers your way.", rather than, "Tick here to grant permission for us to contact you with news and offers."

Preface – If, for legal reasons, the wording cannot be changed, try to preface it with something that makes it sound more human such as "We have to put this rather tedious small print on here for legal reasons. Also, we have to ask you to read it. Sorry about this – our lawyers are absolutely adamant."

Relocate – Hide it in a part of the website which takes a good couple of clicks to reach - clearly signposted of course.

*Writing in plain English
wins more sales*

Location and contact us

These pages should be kept pretty simple, because anyone clicking on them generally wants to get cold, hard facts with no messing around. This is not the place to be waffling on with text like *"Our eco-friendly head office is nestled away in the heart of the New Forest, where a family of woodpeckers can often be heard tapping away during our meetings"*.

In one test by Jakob Nielsen, plain writing improved usability by 27%. Readers also were able to read it faster and remembered more. He conjectures that "promotional language imposes a cognitive burden on users who have to spend resources on filtering out the hyperbole to get at the facts".

Contact us – On this page, people will expect to find the address and phone number as well as an email contact form.

Location page – If this is relevant to your business people expect to find the address and phone number as well. Don't worry about repeating it.

- ◆ *Do put the postcode after your address (yes, there are some websites that don't include it for some reason. That's maddening for the person who has jumped on your site quickly just to get the postcode to key into their sat nav). Make sure the postcode works for sat navs and Google Maps – often they come up with a route that takes you to the wrong place. If necessary include a different, sat nav-friendly postcode or alert your reader to the problem and tell them what they need to know to find you.*

- ◆ *Do make sure the phone number is on every page of your website, not just the Contact Us Page. It's very irritating for a potential customer if they have to hunt around for your phone number. The top right hand corner is a good place for it – this seems to be where people naturally look for it.*

- ◆ *Do include a map, information about opening hours and directions for bus, train and road.*

Environmental policy

Most websites should have an eco section, although many don't. However, they're a good insurance policy for the future. At some point, some of your customers (and possibly a nosy journalist) will want to know your company's stance on green issues, so it's a good idea to have the answers ready for them.

The scope and structure of your environmental policy will be influenced to a large degree by the nature of your business. A large multi-national has many more issues than a little niche company employing half a dozen people, and a business making soft toys has different energy issues from ones making frozen foods.

Another factor is the extent to which your company has already been looking at green issues. If you are enterprising enough to hold an ISO 14001 certificate you will have already worked out your policy on many of the key issues and have measurable targets. In this case your main issue is deciding how best to communicate your efforts simply and clearly.

If your commitment to the environment begins and ends with a separate bin for waste paper there will be a little more analysis needed. It may also involve some soul searching, as your environmental policy statement shouldn't just be a series of platitudes, but a reflection of a genuine commitment within the company.

Your statement should be clear and easy to understand by people within the company and outside, including your customers. The opening needs to summarise the key activities of the company. Don't try to pretend you're whiter than white – every organisation has some impact on the environment. Recognise your shortcomings and try to show that you are doing everything you can and continually trying to improve.

Environmental issues

The next part of your environmental policy looks at the specific areas where your company hopes to improve either by using less or by doing more. Some key areas where you might be trying to reduce your environmental impact are:

- *Energy consumption*
- *Environmental impact of producing products*
- *Use of natural resources*
- *Waste disposal*
- *Transportation*
- *Emissions*
- *Chemical pollutants*
- *Water usage*

Key areas where you could be doing more are:

- *Recycling*
- *Reuse of waste materials*
- *Reuse of energy*
- *Reuse of water*
- *Sustainability of raw materials*

Your statement might also cover areas such as:

- *Staff training in environmental issues*
- *How you work with suppliers to reduce environmental impact and transportation*
- *How you set goals and targets*

In writing your policy, be honest and sincere. Accept your flaws and show how you plan to improve. Try to keep a tone of voice that is in keeping with your brand – don't suddenly adopt a preaching tone just because it's a worthy subject.

The message to your customers is that you are doing as much as you can. Deep down, most consumers don't want to make any great sacrifices themselves, but they do like to know that their suppliers are doing it on their behalf.

Prepare your environmental policy now, before it's required, either by law or some PR crisis. It may not win immediate extra sales, but long term it may help stop some being lost. There may be other hidden benefits too. Many companies, when they start to look at environmental issues, discover that it improves morale and staff retention and that the changes put in place start to save money as well as saving the planet.

Other online copy

Trigger emails

Trigger emails are sent out automatically as a result of some action taken by the website user. (They are second cousin to thrust emails which are sent out by the company irrespective of any action taken by the customer.) Sometimes called 'good dog' emails because they reward the users, they are integral to a successful website. Typical trigger emails include:

- ♦ **Thank you** *for signing up to our newsletter*
- ♦ **Thank you** *for requesting a catalogue*
- ♦ **Thank you** *for placing an order*
- ♦ **Thank you** *for requesting our buyer's guides*
- ♦ **Thank you** *for recommending a friend*
- ♦ **Thank you** *for putting things in our basket – we've saved them for you (Basket abandonment programmes)*

Keep them short, sincere and make it clear why they are receiving it.

Pay per click

This has become pretty much synonymous with Google Adwords. When someone searches a particular word or phrase, your 65 character ad – consisting of headline, two lines of text and your web address – pops up on their screen to the right of the search results. It's become popular because you only pay if someone clicks on your ad. As legendary copywriter Drayton Bird explains, "It's rather like having a stall that sells drinks and that magically appears next to someone when they are thirsty."

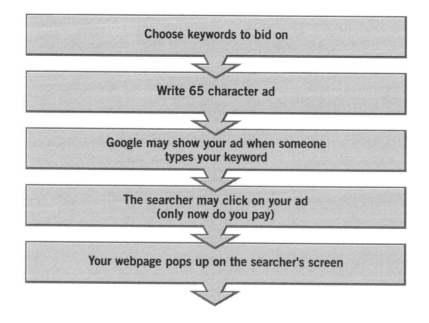

There are now all sorts of variations, such as 'remarketing' where targeted ads appear to people known to have been on your site recently, but the principle is the same.

Choosing pay per click keywords

Choosing the keywords to advertise (or rather, to bid on) is an analytical process rather than a creative one. Often the lower volume, cheaper keywords will win you more clicks. Someone typing in 'Rare Breed Old Spot Pigs for Sale' is likely to be a hotter prospect than someone typing in 'Pigs'. Plus, Google prefers to show ads that they consider most relevant to the search, so if you only sell rare breed old spot pigs, you'll be in with a good chance of your ad coming up. It's a bit like an auction, but one where the auctioneer doesn't award it to the highest bidder, but instead bangs the gavel and says, "Gone to the lower bidder whom I think deserves it the most".

Writing your Adwords

The ad that appears in the search results page (SERPS) does require copywriting, because this is your shot to persuade them to click through to your site. You have only moments to persuade them to do that, so it needs to be really compelling.

You also have very few words in which to do it as Google Adwords' limit of 65 characters only allows a headline and two lines of text. When copy is this short, every word counts. Even something as simple as using 'fast' rather than 'quickly' can make a difference to response.

Designer **Dog** Collars

**Gorgeous canine couture
designed by Lilly.
www.lovemydog.co.uk**

■ Pay Per Click ads (PPC or Google Adwords) are 65 characters long including spaces, plus the web address.

When you're writing or reviewing Adword copy, keep in mind the keyword, and think about what is going on in the mind of the person who has typed in that particular word or phrase. Go for the best benefit you can find – tell your customer exactly what's in it for them. You will need several versions for testing.

Testing Adwords

The only way to know for sure which Adword is best is to test. Always an important part of direct marketing, there is an added incentive here to create a popular ad. Google charge less for Adwords that get clicked more often, so the more effective your ad, the less it will cost you.

When you're writing the copy, always remember to write for one person. Picture them sitting at the computer screen and really try to imagine their feelings, thoughts and motivations. Work on the landing page at the same time as the ad, so you can keep in mind the whole process as the viewer will experience it, and create a cohesive, logical flow for them.

Summary

Web content is critical to the success of a website. Awareness of the purpose and characteristics of each type of copy makes it easier to commission or write in-house and gets more effective results.

Be aware of the functions of, and differences between, the home page, category overviews and product pages.

Write in a conversational style that's easy to read. Reassure your customers every step of the way through calming words and design that works with the copy.

Use every opportunity to reinforce your brand and remember to ask for the sale.

When writing other online copy such as Pay Per Click ads or trigger emails keep in mind the whole process through the eyes of the user.

7 | Web copy and other online media

8 | Catalogue copy and other offline media

Different parts of a catalogue need different types of copy, each with its own characteristics. Typically, copy is needed for:

- ◆ *Front cover*
- ◆ *Welcome message*
- ◆ *Headings and introductions*
- ◆ *Product copy, including information boxes and call-outs*
- ◆ *Advice (eg: fitting instructions)*
- ◆ *Small print*
- ◆ *Covering letter*

Front cover

You have milliseconds to convince someone to open your cover. Every word needs to be crisp, sharp and focussed on giving someone a reason to look inside. Whatever text you put on the cover will have to compete with your logo, strapline, awards, phone number, web address, date or issue number and so on, so there's not much room left.

Ideally you should be looking at a carefully chosen headline and a couple of sub-heads. Every word counts and they need to pack a punch. The aim is to encapsulate the main promise of the entire catalogue, and point to things which are new, improved or on offer. So cover lines for a catalogue selling toys might be:

> *YOUR HAPPIEST SUMMER EVER*
>
> *NEW: Musical Swingball Sets*
>
> *PLUS: 28 new Frisbee designs*

Flicks

The other good thing to put on a front cover is an offer. Use a graphic device for it like a roundel or flash. You don't have to put details of the whole offer – the aim is to give just enough to make someone want to open the cover. So instead of

"Free bag when you buy any pair of shoes costing £65 or more excluding premium suede"

you can just say

"FREE Shoe Bag – see page 2"

It's guaranteed to improve the chances of your catalogue getting opened rather than binned.

What if you don't have any offers? Take a creative look at things like shipping charges. Do you offer free delivery on higher priced orders? If so, then make a feature of this with a roundel saying "FREE DELIVERY on all orders over £50". Or if you offer discounts on some ranges when the customer buys two or three, then your roundel might read "LOOK OUT FOR MULTI-BUY OFFERS".

It may sound obvious, but it's surprising how often good offers get buried deep within the bowels of the catalogue. One company had an agreement that members of a particular charity would get 15% discount, but this fact was casually mentioned at the bottom of the welcome message rather than flagged up on the cover to draw people in.

Another offered a free gift on orders above a certain value, but only mentioned it in a small box on the order form. By the time someone has reached that part of the catalogue, it's too late to gain extra sales from it. The order form is a great place to mention offers as a reminder, but not as an announcement.

It's all about finding a balance. You need enough enticements to persuade your reader to open the cover but not too many messages so that nothing gets read.

Catalogue welcome message

The welcome message usually found on page 2 is similar to an editorial in a magazine. It says "There are real people waiting to help you" (because, as the old saying goes, people buy from people), and makes the catalogue look up to date by talking about something topical. It's also to help people find their way round the catalogue, and reinforce your brand message (why they should buy from you).

One thing it is not is a chance for you to talk about yourself. Customers are only interested in one thing – themselves. Always write for the reader and their interests and aim to use the words 'you' and 'your' twice as often as 'we' or 'our'. Watch out for phrases like these – if you spot too many in your copy it's time for a re-write...

♦ *We're so delighted with our new catalogue...*

♦ *We've worked really hard to produce this year's catalogue...*

- *So many people have told us it's a great catalogue...*
- *We're keeping our fingers crossed that we're going to win lots of awards*
- *We've won loads of awards...*
- *It's been a wonderful year for us all here...*
- *I hope we have succeeded in exceeding our customers' expectations...*
- *Our aspiration is to grow our business, and we pride ourselves on...*
- *We are one of the most successful...*

Instead tell the customers what's in it for them. Turn everything round into a positive for them. "Your biggest ever choice", "New easier-to-use layout" and so on. Try not to make the welcome message too long. Firstly, this part of the catalogue doesn't really sell, (it just supports the sales process) and secondly it rarely gets read closely. What people notice is a photo and signature; these two elements alone can create a feeling of trust that helps to put them in the mood for buying.

Mention 'you' or 'your' more than 'we' or 'us'

Spread headings and introductions

Because catalogues are viewed as 'spreads' ie: two pages at a time, they are best planned as spreads too. Products with a similar theme can be grouped together, and the headings and introductions help to make it easier for the customer to find their way around.

A heading can be as simple as a generic description such as 'Bedrooms', 'Bed linen' or 'Sheets'. In that sense it's similar to a category heading on a website. However, in catalogues there's also room for a little more creativity as you're not restricted by keywords. Because people are browsing and expecting to be entertained and inspired, the headings may be written around a general feeling, or concept, such as 'Sweet Dreams' or 'Drift off to sleep in finest Egyptian Cotton'.

On websites each category would normally have a paragraph or two of copy, as 'spider food' to increase your search engine rankings. In catalogues, copy is only needed when there is something important to be explained that's common to every product on the spread.

Say you have a spread of bed linen, all made from the same type of fabric. You could write something like, "All our pure cotton sheets feel incredibly smooth and silky-soft, because they have a 600 thread count. That's twice as many threads per square inch as standard cotton." This saves repeating it in each individual piece of copy. That's a better use of space and more interesting for the reader. However, if the products on the spread have no common features, it's better to do away with the intro copy and use the space for a bigger hero photo or an extra product.

Product copy

Your product copy is absolutely critical to your business, because this is where the sale is made. Everything else – all your fabulous photography, art direction, beautiful print, and clever segmentation of your database is all designed to get people to read this copy and decide to buy.

The ideal piece of product copy is similar to a mini advertisement. Just like an ad, it needs a headline to attract attention and explain the key benefit, body copy which explains all the features and benefits and a call to action so that the reader knows how to buy it.

That structure is also the same as product copy on the website. It will read differently because keywords have to be included and the format may be different (with lots of the bullet points and sub-heads that search engines love) but the principles are exactly the same.

Product copy headline

The secret of creating a compelling headline is to talk about the benefit, not the feature. Tell the customer what the product will do for them (not what the product does). A speed reading course will "Double your learning power". A gadget to stop your freezer icing up promises you can "End the chore of defrosting". It's the difference between what you are selling and what your customer is buying.

This is far more important than trying to come up with something clever or witty. The right message put across plainly will always do better than a sparkling headline with the wrong message. (Although it's always worth trying not to be dull. Boring people isn't usually a good way to sell to them.)

Lead with your best benefit

Sometimes there might be so much to say about your product that it's hard to decide what to go for. The temptation may be to try and cram in everything, but resist this with all your might. It's a recipe for a weak headline that won't pull in anyone. As I mentioned in Chapter 6, always start with your most compelling benefit. If you could only tell your customer one thing what would it be?

This formula for a winning headline has been successfully used for donkey's years. Here's an advertisement from the 1920s for the Blue Bird Electric Clothes Washer. Did the headline describe the precision-engineered components of the machine, the quality of the steel used to make the drum or compare the thoroughness of the wash to hand-washing? No, it led on the emotional benefit of "HAPPY HANDS" with a sub-head "never tired or reddened by washday", with a big photo of a pretty lady staring with delight and wonderment at her unblemished hands.

However, the best benefit can change – after all, no washing machine ad would run with a headline like that nowadays, because things have moved on. Victoria Laws of Scotts

& Co says that this is especially important for continuity lines that don't change from season to season. "Copy and imagery gets stale and at certain times different product benefits mean more than at other times. For example, when electricity prices are sky high, energy-saving features suddenly became massively important."

Bullet points and call-outs

A key plank of your product copy strategy is using bullet points and call outs. These two devices are an excellent way to communicate the message more effectively and save valuable space. They are also useful where you have two or three similar products, as it makes it easy for customers to compare one against another.

Use bullet points where you have a number of short, simple features which in copy would be little more than a list. This is quite different from bullets in a website, which are carefully chosen to express the main benefits.

Call-outs are inset photos and text designed to draw attention to special features. They are especially good for technical products, as the small photo and caption is often the easiest way to explain a complex feature. The illustration (right) from Muddy Puddles is a good example of the use of both call-outs and bullet points.

Advice copy in catalogues

Sometimes you need to educate your customers to be able to persuade them to buy. For example if you sell hats they may need instructions on how to measure their head.

On websites, content like this is perfect to help give your site relevance and authority to help your natural search rankings. In catalogues it's a nuisance, as it takes up valuable space that could be used for selling products. Even worse, it can put your potential customer off buying by making it look as though buying your product is complicated or a hassle.

Take a long hard look at your advice copy and pare it back to the bare minimum. A lot of catalogues include information which isn't needed until the product has been purchased. If you're selling a kitchen extractor fan, you might have to explain how to take some key measurements (so they can order the right size) but not include a detailed wiring diagram, as that can wait until they actually receive the product. You can also refer people to your website for more detailed information, rather than use up space in the catalogue.

Anything you do decide to include should be designed and written to look easy. Break it down into small steps and use arrows and boxes to help guide them through the process. The copy can support it with short, upbeat statements like "It's so easy to measure…" and "To find the size you need simply …"

Catalogue small print

Nearly every catalogue, brochure and leaflet has to have some sort of small print. However there's nothing more off-putting than a dense block of text that looks like a contract. The art of copywriting small print is threefold: **Reduce**, **Rewrite**, **Restructure**.

Reduce – Go through and cut out as much as possible. Unless there is a legal reason why it has to stay in, get rid of it.

Rewrite – Can any negative be turned into a positive? Small print such as "To return an item, you must send it back in its original packaging within 21 days", can be turned around to read, "You have a full three weeks to change your mind. Just return your unused goods in their original packaging for a full refund."

Restructure – Look at what there is left. Anything which is a positive benefit for the customer should be made more prominent. The remaining negative small print can be split up and dotted throughout the catalogue to dilute the effect. For example, a disclaimer about reserving the right to substitute could be put in the corner of page two while the data protection disclaimer can go on the order form. This avoids having heavy blocks of small print that makes your customer's heart sink.

Covering letter

It's sometimes said that the letter sells the catalogue and the catalogue sells the product. Of course, that's only true if the letter is on the outside of your catalogue. If it's on the inside, you're relying on the cover alone to entice your customer in. Adding a sales letter doubles your chances as you've got two elements working for you instead of just one.

A separate sales letter can make the most of your database, as it's a great place to make targeted offers. You can also use it to build a relationship by addressing different types of customer in different ways. Your best customers get a more intimate, personal letter with insider knowledge, tips and views. Meanwhile your weaker customers may need something that reminds them of all the great reasons to buy (expressed in terms of benefits for them – not you!) If you want proof that these letters get read, then just send one out with a time-limited offer that's only mentioned in the letter, and look out for the spike in orders just before the closing date.

Over the last few years, fewer and fewer catalogues have been sent out with a covering letter, especially since the dawn of naked mailings (catalogues mailed with no envelope). However, in test after test, a covering letter increases sales beyond the cost of the letter. Ladies fashion retailer Eric Hill has tested sending catalogues out both with and without the letter, and found that for every £100 extra the letter costs, it generates an extra £200 in sales.

Success depends on a number of factors including the offer, target audience, the wording and the look of the letter, so there are no guarantees it will work every time. However, it's certainly worth testing.

Summary

Focussed copy helps your catalogue perform better. Be aware of the function of copy for different parts of your catalogue.

Every product should be written like a mini- advertisement

Use introductory copy to describe features and benefits that are common to all products on the spread.

Use bullets and call-outs to save space and aid clarity.

8 | # Catalogue copy and other offline media

9 | **Testing and research**

Testing is suddenly sexy again – thanks to the rise of online marketing. In those ancient far off times before we had the internet, fortunes were made in direct marketing by rigorously testing the effectiveness of mailings and advertisements. However, the riches were hard-earned as the number-crunching exercises were often tedious and longwinded.

Today it's all so much easier. Google Analytics, with its smart dashboards and fancy coloured charts have made it fashionable to look at the figures – at least, the online figures. Although in a strange irony, it seems as though the easier it is to get hold of the information the less we make use of it. "Digital is measurable, but that doesn't mean it's effective." says Tony Leach, Logistics General Manager at Debenhams. "It's not enough just to look at the data, you have to act on it."

Testing is still the only way to find out what really works for your business. In direct marketing a small difference can really give you the edge, both on and offline. For example, say you find that every time you mail a particular offer to a particular list, you get 1% response. To get a response rate of 1.5% you only need to get one person in every two hundred to respond who wouldn't have done otherwise. A jump from 1% to 1.5% is a 50% increase in turnover – for no extra cost.

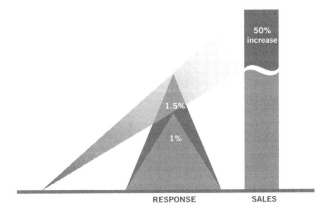

The other great thing to bear in mind with testing is that it is reasonably predictable. If you get a particular result once, statistically you will get the same result again if you repeat it in the same way. In the nineteenth century Lord Leverhulme, founder of Unilever said, "I know that half the money I spend on advertising is wasted – I just don't know which half". Testing means you can know which half (or more likely, which 98%) is going to waste – and there are now a whole raft of tools and techniques available to find out the answer.

A/B split tests – the basis of testing

Want to know if changing the headline will win you more sales? Or if replacing a product shot with a smiling face will raise your revenue? If adding a word to your subject line will get more click-thrus? The answer is a split test.

Once the bedrock of every successful direct marketing business, split testing is now becoming the stock-in-trade of e-commerce websites. It's very simple and the principles are the same for both online and offline. You create two versions and present viewers with either one or the other. You then record their behaviour and see which one works best. Then you do it again putting the 'winner' head-to-head against a new test to see if you can create something else that will outperform the control. Eventually you create a virtuous circle of constantly improving sales and riches.

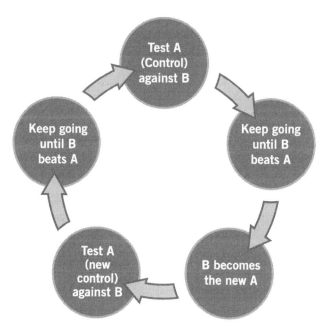

■ The 'Virtuous Circle' of testing.

A/B split testing has been used for a couple of centuries to hone and refine print ads, inserts, mailing packs, posters and even TV ads and radio commercials. It can also be used for online media including websites and landing pages, emails and banner ads.

Although it's called an A/B test, you don't have to be limited to just two items. As long as the sample size is big enough, this principle can be applied to several items at once and is known as multivariate testing.

When you're structuring your test matrix, you need a 'banker', a control piece that always performs well. This should be the lion's share of the promotion, with much smaller sample sizes for the test (or tests). It is very risky to use an unproven piece. They could do well or badly, so they should only be rolled out after the results are in.

If you're split testing a website, then you can choose what percentage of traffic sees the new landing page – it doesn't have to be a 50/50 split. To reduce the risk, you can fix things so that 90% of visitors see the old page. The only drawback to this is that results take longer to come in.

It may sound like common sense to put a toe in the water by running a test before spending a lot of money on a whole campaign. In real life, though, it's easy to become enchanted by the new creative work and convinced it will have people ordering in droves. Although everyone hopes that the tests are going to pull better than the control, no-one ever knows for sure until after the event. I'm embarrassed to tell you how many times I've tried to guess the winner in a split test, and picked the dud. And I'm not alone. What's surprising is how often experienced marketers fare no better at predicting results than just sticking in a pin blindfolded. So always hold fire on sending out huge quantities until you have some data.

Setting up an A/B test

The stages in setting up an A/B split test are:

a) **Planning**

- *What elements are to be tested?*
- *How big will the sample be?*
- *What will be the time period for the test?*
- *How will the results be monitored and put into practice?*

b) **Testing**

- *Conducting the tests and gathering the results*

c) **Analysis**

- *Which did best?*
- *Was it statistically significant?*

d) **Implementation**

- *Incorporating the new creative treatment that 'beat the control' (or not)*

e) **Planning for the next round of testing**

Guiding principles for A/B testing

Some of the guiding principles for website A/B split tests are exactly the same as traditional direct marketing including:

Test one element of the design or the copy at a time. Eg: change the headline or the offer or the background colour but not all of them at once. If you change two or three items, you don't know which one of them makes the difference, so you learn nothing. Known as the 'single variable' test, it allows you to pinpoint exactly what is making the difference. The only exception to this is to test everything, known as 'breakthrough testing' where you would test two completely different creative treatments – the more diverse the better.

Test something meaningful. Testing a different type of free gift is meaningful, but testing different bullet point shapes on a bullet-pointed list is not. If you're not sure whether something is meaningful, then my grandma, a down-to-earth Yorkshire-woman, has the perfect piece of advice for you, *"Use the common sense you were born with".*

Make sure the sample sizes are big enough to be statistically significant. The good thing about testing is that it's possible to work out the mathematical probability that the roll-out will perform as well as the test. However, you do need enough orders for one of the tests to emerge as a clear winner. To be able to do the calculations with a degree of certainty, you generally need around 100-150 orders from the test programme, which could mean a sample mailing of 5,000 catalogues or mailshots and possibly more for an email broadcast.

Record your results in a 'guard book'. At one time 'guard books' were the golden assets of successful direct marketing companies. Even in our digital age, you will do well to keep a hard copy of every single test. It's a simple admin job, and all it takes is a few lever arch files to keep a sample of each catalogue and mailing pack, or hard copy of every email and web page change together with a record of the key facts.

The advantage of keeping paper records is that it's so much quicker and easier to look back and see exactly what was done. It's very hard to get a real feel for an offline promotion just looking at a pdf on screen. You need to have the paper catalogue in your hands, together with any other elements that went with it, such as a letter or polythene wrap to get a true reflection of what the customer experienced.

On the next page are suggested 'Guard Book Records' to fill in and file with a record of each promotion.

GUARD BOOK (Catalogue Mailings)

Campaign period   _____

Drop date   _____

Target   _____

Offers   _____

Quantity mailed   _____

Total sales   £ _____

No of orders   _____

Response rate   _____ %

Commentary _____

_____

_____

_____

_____

BENCHMARKING

Average order value   £ _____
(Total sales £ ÷ total no of orders)

Cost of mailing   £ _____

Cost per order   £ _____
(Cost of mailing ÷ total no of orders)

Sales per '000 mailed   £ _____
(Total sales £ ÷ total no mailed x 1000)

Sales per £1,000 investment   £ _____
(Total sales £ ÷ cost of mailing x 1000)

GUARD BOOK (emails)

Campaign period   _____

Broadcast date   _____

Format   _____

Target   _____

Offers/Theme   _____

Quantity emailed   _____

Bounce rate   _____

Opened   _____

Clicked thru   _____

Sales £   _____

Response rate   _____ %

Offline mailing in same period YES/NO

BENCHMARKING

Average order value   £ _____
(Total sales £ ÷ total no of orders)

Cost of emailing   £ _____

Cost per order   £ _____
(Cost of emailing ÷ total no of orders)

Sales per '000 emailed   £ _____
(Total sales £ ÷ total no emailed x 1000)

Sales per £1,000 investment   £ _____
(Total sales £ ÷ cost of emailing x 1000)

Act on the results. This may sound blindingly obvious. After all, why wouldn't you? It's the key to getting a better result next time. But what often happens is that once the test is done and dusted it gets forgotten about. It's important to keep the guard books up to date, monitor the results and share them with the team so that everyone is motivated towards constant improvement.

Other reasons why the results don't get acted on is that they get misread, or simply not believed. It's human nature to think that the one we like the best is the one everyone will respond to – despite what the numbers tell us.

What elements can be tested?

There are almost limitless opportunities to test different elements, but you've got to start somewhere – so what's best to test? The answer depends partly on what elements you've tested already. It makes sense to test new elements rather than endlessly refine things you've already tried. But if you're starting from scratch, then the first tests should be geared towards things you think will make the most difference and getting some benchmarks established.

Here are some ideas for starters. Remember, these are broad principles, and can be adapted and applied to pretty much all your online and offline marketing material.

Media/Target audience

Who you pitch your offer to is the second most important factor after the offer itself. It's therefore extremely valuable to find out which lists and publications and affiliate websites work best for you. Run the same email, mailing shot etc to different lists, banner ads on different websites, and press ads and inserts in different magazines. Test out the same offer on Twitter, Facebook and other social media sites. This will tell you immediately which ones are more effective for your business.

Size

Try a smaller page count. It used to be a truism that more pages won you more sales. However, times are changing. Kevin Hillstrom, President of MineThatData cites an example where a catalogue with just 48 pages pulled in 98% of the sales of a 148 page catalogue. He recommends testing to find out just how small your catalogue can go. Reducing the number of pages costs less to produce and to mail, which frees up money to spend on mailing other customers, or simply mailing more often.

Segmentation

As soon as your own customer database is large enough, you should segment it into different target audiences. Among the people who have bought from you there will be some who are high spenders, buying frequently and others who hardly ever buy or never

spend much. Talking to them in different ways (with different offers) will yield better results than treating them all the same.

How you group your customers depends to a large extent on how many you have. When you're a small company with just a few thousand names on your database, then a very simple segmentation will be good enough (best, good and lapsed for example). When your database gets into the hundreds of thousands, you may have a dozen or so different segments, each one based on common buying patterns and other profile data.

Incentive offers

Many experts believe that the offer is the second most important factor in the success of any promotion, just behind the target audience.

The offer is a proposal to your customer or prospect: You will receive X in return for taking the action Y. (Typically X is some goods or a service and the Y action is buying the goods or service for a certain price from a particular place by a specified date with or without additional incentives such as a free gift.)

An offer does not always have to be a free gift or a discount, although you might well find (through testing) that there is a psychological price point that works for your business when it comes to acquiring new customers.

Here are some of the most tried and tested offers, proven to get results over and over again.

Personalised offers

Offers based on the actual buying habits of the person you're targeting can produce incredible results. If you sold someone a vacuum cleaner three months ago, they're an ideal prospect for vacuum cleaner bags.

Ian Morrison of Donald Russell cites the example of a poultry offer to people who had previously bought poultry. "Sales were not just ten percent better but 100%", he said.

Cotton Traders have found similar success. In one test, offering suede shoes to previous purchasers of the same product, the mailing produced a response nearly four times better than a non-personalised mailing to the same target audience.

The key to this kind of approach is to recognise in the copy that the offer is specifically for them as a previous customer. Keep the tone very personal and use the person's name throughout, not just in the salutation.

Free delivery offers

In tests, this consistently comes out top, even out-beating offers which save more money. Why does it work so well? For some reason people always resent paying for delivery. When a customer has made up their mind to buy something, they want to buy it at that price. The thought of paying any more makes some people lose interest.

Free gift offers

This is one of those classic examples where what people say and what they do are two completely different things. Of course, everyone tells you that there's no way they would be persuaded to buy something they didn't want just because it came with a free pair of sunglasses or a free tea towel. Yet millions of products from holidays to shoes have been sold in just this way.

Even more erroneous is the view that wealthy individuals are somehow less likely to fall for such a tawdry gimmick, when in fact the reverse is often true. It's simple human nature. As cavemen, if we saw something tasty lying around we were programmed to scoop it up and take it back to our dwelling place. That's how the race has survived.

Your gifts should have a high perceived value

What makes the ideal free gift? Firstly it should have a high perceived value, or be intrinsically valuable to the recipient. Free books, e-books, white papers and factsheets that have information that your potential customer really wants to know can be a great vehicle for gaining leads and sales.

Over the last few years glossy magazines on the newsstands have been giving away products attached to the cover. Often the products themselves are nothing special – a canvas bag or a skimpy T-shirt. The added value comes from being emblazoned with some sort of designer logo.

Which brings me to the second point, that the gift should be relevant to your brand. It's absolutely spot-on for a fashion magazine to offer a mirror branded with the name of a make-up artist, but wide of the mark if you are selling screwdrivers or sports gear.

A relative of the free gift is to offer to gift-wrap your products (or include a personalised gift message). This has the double whammy of both helping to gain a sale and introducing your brand to a potential new customer (the lucky person who receives the gift).

In recent times we have seen the re-emergence of an old favourite that had its heyday in the 1970s – the mystery gift. This can work surprisingly well – people are naturally curious. They're also highly cynical, so if you want to win them over to become long-term customers, surprise and delight them with a gift that's better than they might have expected.

The free gift can be a reward for buying any product from the website or just for a selected range. It can also be a good way to get your customers to spend more, by offering the free gift only on orders above a certain value. Depending on your sales process you might want to give the gift just for trying the product (they get to keep the gift even if they send the product back) or for making an enquiry or giving you their email address. It depends how valuable their custom is to your particular business.

Other freebies

Free is a powerful, attention grabbing word. Here are some other things you can offer for free:

- *Free prize draw*
- *Free trial*
- *Free refills*
- *Free sample*
- *Free report*
- *Free consultation*
- *Free assessment*
- *Free check up*
- *Free bonus points (eg: if you already have a loyalty scheme)*

Price

Price is a key element, and worth testing separately from offers (where the price is just one element of the total package). Test both high and low prices – the results could surprise you. Victoria Laws, Group Buying Director at Scotts & Co says, "Never just assume your price should be cost plus margin. Knowing when to take a better margin is as important as knowing when to cut it. A higher priced product sometimes does better because it hits the sort of price point people are looking to pay or it's perceived as better quality. Even if it brings in a lower number of orders it can still be more profitable because of the extra margins."

Price presentation

You can also test different ways of presenting the same price. For example, a lot of products lend themselves to being sold in boxed sets, including food, drink, and beauty products.

A presentation pack of cleanser, toner, moisturiser, eye make-up remover and face pack could be presented as "£45 – save £5". Or it could be sold at "£45 plus FREE Face Pack". Which one will work best? Experience suggests the free gift will outperform the saving, even though the price is exactly the same.

Other price offers include:

Cross-sells - Offering a complementary product at a reduced price (eg: half price tie with every shirt).

Upsells - Offering a selection of products at a reduced price with any purchase from the main range.

Buy One Get One Free - (affectionately known as BOGOF) is always a good one to test as it usually does better than 'half price', '50% off' or 'two for the price of one' even though they are all essentially the same offer.

Timing

The date and time a promotion goes out has always been a big factor in its success. Certain seasons (like the run up to Christmas) or particular months can be much better than others. Some of my clients have found that a Tuesday, Thursday or Sunday do better, and Gavin Ucko of The Happy Puzzle Company says a dull, dry weekend is good for business. "When it's sunny people go off and do things, and when it's wet they don't want to leave the house, but when it's cloudy but not raining, they're happy to trundle down to the newsagents then go back home and read the paper."

The rise of the internet has made timing even more critical, and shortened the time frame from months to weeks, days or even down to certain hours of the day being better than others. Social media offers sometimes do better going out at night when people are at home. Although they can usually view the offers at work, they probably can't act on them. Testing will tell you what works best for your business.

Frequency

Closely allied to timing is frequency ie: how often your ad appears, your email goes out, your home page is changed, your sales letters and catalogues are mailed. Most retailers hugely underestimate the amount of times you can get in touch with your customers. Sending something out every six weeks or less is not nearly enough. Neiman Marcus, for example, sends an email almost every day.

Experiment with contacting people more frequently (especially email which is relatively cheap) and see what happens. After all, they have given you permission to get in touch. Even if your emails don't get opened, there's a good chance that they are still wanted. Nowadays it's common for people to be on several email lists. They like being able to pick and choose which ones to open.

Make it very, very easy to unsubscribe and put it at the top, not the bottom of the email. It's better to have your reader unsubscribe than letting them consign you to the junk folder, because then you can get in touch to find out why they want to stop hearing from you. You could pick up some useful insights, and possibly even win them back as a customer, but if you get junked, you're out of their orbit forever.

Geography

If your business is local you may just want to advertise in the area around you, but even then you'll probably find some streets perform much better than others. National businesses often find that parts of the country are much better than others.

Visuals

Changing the colour, the position of the headline or the font can make a difference. Colour is particularly important on the web, where yellow and orange act on the brain's limbic system to induce fear, which can directly reduce the number of conversions you get from the site. Some clients have found that changing their 'basket' icon to a graphic of a supermarket trolley has improved conversions, even if it's still called a 'basket' – the preferred word for UK websites.

In print media, there have been dozens of tests showing that a serif font for your body copy rather than a sans serif improves response.

(Serif is one that has little tails on the end of the letters like Times New Roman ... **rather than a plain minimalist font like Arial**).

In these tests, literally every single part of the ad, sales letter or mailing pack is exactly the same, so it has to be the font that makes the difference.

Large chunks of coloured text tend to depress response. Reversed out text (eg: white text on a black or coloured background) is also surprisingly tricky to read. You certainly can't get the meaning in a single glance, and text set like this also gets lower responses than exactly the same content black on white. (One exception to this is theatre programmes where the dim lighting makes reversed out text easier to read.)

Other small changes to the visuals that can have a surprisingly big effect include moving the headline to a different place, increasing the size of your photos and putting captions under photos. (According to eye-tracking research, captions are one of the most read parts of a page, so putting a key sales message here can be very effective.)

Photography

The role of the photograph is to grab attention and make the product look so inviting that the viewer is stopped in their tracks to find out more. It does this through a combination of good lighting and excellent technical skills, as well as styling that's relevant to the brand. However, by itself that may not be enough to make the sale. Look at it through your customers' eyes. Having got them interested, are the details clear enough to make a decision? Is there a prop obscuring a key feature of the photo? Does it need close-ups of particular parts of the product (especially if it's a complex, high-priced item)?

Other experiments you can make with photography include adding in a baby (yes really. Terribly cheesy, but when it's relevant it can increase response), making sure that models are looking into camera (ie: out at the reader) rather than looking away, and keeping photos clear of text. And if in doubt, make your photos bigger, especially if they show your bestsellers.

Styling can make a significant difference. In the last decade or so, some of the more successful catalogues are the ones which have introduced lifestyle photographs as well as product shots. Furniture shown as a room set laid up for dinner, possibly with attractive people enjoying themselves... mountaineering equipment featuring a close-up of a guy's face twisted with exertion as he scales a mountainside. These kind of images are proving astonishingly successful, because they allow people to buy into the dream. It's a technique that successful TV commercials have used for decades.

Technology

Several companies have reported great results with emails that show products that click straight through to the website, or even an interactive catalogue.

On the other hand, some companies are getting excellent opening rates with plain-text emails. No fancy graphics, just a good old-fashioned message, a bit like you would send to your friends. (Perhaps that's why they work so well – because it does feel like a message from a good friend.)

Testing a letter with your catalogue

There are dozens of tests that show that a catalogue sent with a letter gets more orders than one without, although the additional cost may make them less profitable overall. Craft your letter well, using the AIDA framework (Attention, Interest, Desire and Action), giving all the benefits and asking for the sale.

Break the letter up with sub-heads to highlight key benefit and a PS. The PS is the second most read part of the letter (after the person's name) so use it to re-state the offer. You can repeat the person's name in the PS too.

Use sub-heads and photographs to break up the layout, but make sure your letter looks like a letter, with paper that looks like a proper letterhead and a signature that's specially art directed to look in keeping with the brand personality. (It can be based on the MD's real signature, but should be significantly different to help prevent identity theft).

Copy

They say "The photo tells, the copy sells" so it can be useful to hone your words by changing the copy and keeping everything else the same. The key thing is to make a change that is substantially different from the control (and one that you think may do better). You can change just one part (such as the headline or email subject line or re-write the whole lot. Which route you go depends on whether the different parts still work together. If you have a new headline can the copy stand as is, or does it need to be amended to follow on? Here are some ideas for testing:

Try a different headline

Donald Russell tested two headlines on an insert to try and attract new customers. They were identical in every way, except one had the headline "Love Me Tender" and the other had "You've Never Tasted Better Beef". The latter outperformed the play on words by a factor of two to one. Often emotion-based headlines do very well, but in this instance the benefit-led headline won.

Try turning your basic headline into a question. "New superfood helps you lose five pounds in a week" could become "Would you like to try a new superfood – and lose five pounds in a week?" You can also write it as a command, "Try this new superfood – and lose five pounds in a week".

See if there's something else you can add. One client was selling a gadget described as an 'Electronic dictionary'. When that was changed to 'Electronic dictionary and thesaurus', sales shot up.

Try personalising the cover lines on your catalogue using digital printing and special messages with the customer's name in.

Change the benefit

See if you can lead with a different benefit. For example, if you're selling a chemical spray that keeps windows clean for a year, and also puts a UV filter on the glass, you could lead with either:

♦ *"No more washing windows – for a whole year"*
 or

♦ *"End fading pictures – invisible UV filter prevents sun damage'*

Solar-powered products such as lights or a fountain can be headlined as 'eco-friendly' or 'no fuss installation', or 'works forever without batteries'. It's a matter of judgement based on who your target audience is and their needs, fears, hopes and aspirations at the time.

Email subject line/opening line for social media feeds

This is an instant medium, so adding words that bring a freshness or immediacy can bring good results, such as:

♦ *Out now*
♦ *New study*
♦ *Just in*
♦ *Just arrived*
♦ *Fresh today*

Time limited offers also work well, again because of the immediacy of the medium:

- *2 hours only*
- *Ending today...*
- *One day only*
- *You have just 3 hours*

As with headlines, try re-phrasing as a question

- *Have you seen...?*

Remember that people buy from people, so successful subject lines often sound like the sort of subject line you would write to your friends:

- *Great new swimsuit*
- *When are you free?*
- *Thought you might like this*

One of the great things about emails is that you can get two bites at the cherry. If someone hasn't opened your email after three days, just send it again with a different subject line.

Long copy v short copy

Test after test has shown that longer copy outperforms shorter copy. And client after client has disputed this with statements like "no one reads long copy". The problem is not long copy but boring copy. If this is something you plan to test then plan and write it as long copy. Use the words to tell the whole story and draw the customer in – don't simply flesh out a shorter version with meaningless words. One client has even tested long-copy emails, and found (to all our surprise) that the longer versions out-performed the shorter ones – even when announcing the sale.

Body copy

There's no point re-writing your copy just for the sake of it, but it's certainly worth trying if you think sales can be improved. With body copy, the trick is to take a good look at the existing copy and ask questions like:

- *Is the main benefit the first thing mentioned?*
- *Are all the features expressed as benefits?*
- *Are there any other key features not mentioned?*
- *Does it begin with a negative word such as 'Unlike....' or 'Don't...'*
- *Is the tone of voice impersonal and distant?*
- *Does it end with a call to action?*

Asking questions like this can highlight whether there is scope for a copy rewrite that could make a significant difference to response.

4. CARINA WRAP-AROUND SHAWL
by **Georgina B.**
This sophisticated wrap has the feel of cashmere at a fraction of the price, and it doesn't have to be dry-cleaned. It's specially shaped to drape over your shoulders, and is very generously cut with ample folds of luxurious knit fabric. Ideal for travel, evening wear, or even at home when you fancy spoiling yourself while you're watching TV.
• One size
• Length 32" approx
• 100% polyacrylic "cashmere-like"
• Colours: Red or Black
  (see page 14)
Style 120   £45.00

■ The original copy for this product began "Unlike many shawls, this is not simply an oversized scarf..." and wasn't selling. It was later re-written, with an opening line of "This sophisticated wrap has the feel of cashmere at a fraction of the price" and sold out within a few weeks.

Choosing what to test

The ideas above probably cover most of the biggies that you might want to test, but of course, the list is endless. A small word of warning though, before you go rushing full pelt into a complicated testing programme. Make sure that you have the resources to make sense of the results. It's so easy to get carried away by all the different variables you could test that you end up just drowning in data and can't actually put the information to good use.

Before you go ahead, look at your test matrix. If you think it's going to be too much to manage, cut the number of tests this time, and put them on the list for the next round of testing.

Why tests sometimes bomb

Ok, you did everything right. Used a control, tested one variable and got the boffins to check that the uplift was statistically valid. Then you rolled it out and it flopped. Why?

Unfortunately, testing is only a way of reducing the risks, not eliminating them. Here's some possible reasons why it doesn't always go the way you expect:

- *The test somehow wasn't a true representation of the larger list. (Maybe you were inadvertently sent a load of names from the recent buyers list, but the main list has many names who haven't bought for years.)*

- *The sample size was too small to be statistically robust.*

- *There was a big time gap between the test and the roll-out, so seasonality may start to come into play.*

- *The test was small (say, 5,000) and the roll-out was large (say, 100,000+). Often, the roll-out performs less well than the test.*

- *Your competitors may have had another promotion on at a similar time.*

- *Some element of the offer or creative work was different. Testing mail shots requires an obsessive attention to detail. Overlook nothing.*

- *You didn't keep good enough records. It's vital to keep your guard books up to date.*

- *You tested a letter and it appeared to have no better results than the same mailing without a letter. Firstly, was the letter interesting? Did it have a strong message and finish with a call to action or did it passively say something like "Here's your catalogue, hope you like it". Did it look like a letter or was it printed on thin, cheap paper with so many computer codes on it that it looked like a tax demand? Test after test has shown that letters work, (and long letters work even better), so it may be a question of just finding the right letter for your business.*

- *There was some sort of external event. Believe it or not, when Pope John Paul II died, sales plummeted for several of my clients until the new Pope was finally anointed.*

- *Maybe it's something so simple that you've been blinded to the obvious. Perhaps it's time for some research.*

Research

When I look back on my days in advertising agencies working mainly on TV, radio and press ads, I'm struck by how often we used market research. Not a month would go by without some sort of focus group to observe or debrief presentation to attend. We pored over market reports by Mintel, Nielsen and Keynote.

By contrast, in more than ten years of working with home shopping companies, I've only come across three instances of conventional qualitative research. Yet the value was immense. The research revealed customer insights that led to far-reaching changes in strategy and a fundamental shift in brand positioning which continues successfully to this day. Not only did the research pave the way for the new approach, it also gave the management team the clarity, vision and confidence to push it through.

Qualitative research, such as focus groups, is a specialised skill and usually best handled by a market research firm. However, there is still a lot that can be done in-house.

Surveys and questionnaires

One of the great advantages of selling direct is the close relationship you have with your customers. Simply listening in at the call centre, reading your forums or Twitter dialogues or chatting to the customer services team gives you a wealth of information.

One of the easiest ways to do research in-house is to simply ask your customers. There are so many ways to do this, from website questionnaires, a printed survey with every product sent out, or simply phoning up your customers. The main thing is to be crystal clear about what you really want to know, because this will shape the questions you ask. All too often, questions are framed in such a way that the information they reveal is of little use to future decision making.

Framing your questions

There are a number of ways to structure the questions in your surveys:

- *Yes/No*
- *Scoring (eg: On a scale of 1-10 how would you rate... How strongly would you agree or disagree with this statement...?)*
- *Rank-order (eg: Which of these attributes would you rate as most important...?)*
- *Multiple choice*
- *Open ended*

Make your questionnaire as short as possible; the longer it is the fewer responses you will get back. Keep the wording neutral so as not to bias results. Remember your brand values and adopt a conversational tone of voice that fits with your brand personality.

Simple scoring and multiple choice are quickest and easiest for people to answer and for you to collate and analyse the data. However, they can give you a skewed picture, because it may be that the heart of the issue is something that you haven't asked about or haven't included in the list. For that reason it's always good to include some open-ended questions.

Always conduct a pilot study to make sure that the questionnaire or survey is workable and will give you some useful data. Analysing your pilot responses will also give you a feel for how you can present the results, share the findings amongst the team and use it to make future decisions.

Website usability research

Another type of research that can be done quickly and easily in-house (or outsourced for very little cost), is usability testing. How many times have you sat down and tried to order something from a website and thought "aghh...why won't it let me do this?" or "It would be so much better if ..." ?

Almost certainly you're looking at a site where the owner has never watched one of their customers use the site for real and asked them questions like "Why did you click there?" "What did you think would happen?" This is the simplest form of usability testing, and it's incredibly revealing.

How to do usability testing

You need surprisingly few people to get decent results, and unlike most qualititative research it's not hugely important that they are a good match for your customer profile. According to usability experts like Steve Krug and Jakob Nielsen, even as few as five to eight people will tell you 80% of what's wrong with the site, and even just one informal usability test is better than doing none at all.

You can usually find people to take part by recruiting from your own customer database and newsletter list or put an appeal on your website. You start off the session by making the tester feel welcome, and explain that it's the site that's being tested, not them, so it doesn't matter if they make a mistake. (In fact it's often the mistakes that reveal the most.)

The kind of things you might ask them to do are:

- *Where would you click on this home page?*
- *What do you think the website is about? What is it offering?*
- *What do you understand by this message here?*
- *What do you think this part of the website is for?*
- *Can you try and buy a personalised gift to be delivered on Thursday?*

You can download free sample scripts for DIY usability testing from Steve Krug's website, **www.sensible.com**.

Like all research, planning is key. Start by focussing on what you really want to know. Only then can you start to formulate the questions and tasks. Once you've got your framework try not to make it like a script, but keep the focus on getting to the heart of the issue. When you're ready to start your tests, do a few pilot usability studies first to iron out any glitches and check that you are going to get something worthwhile from it. You can also video the sessions for other people on your team to watch.

Remote usability testing

It's also possible to outsource this type of research, with lots of options from expensive laboratories offering detailed insights to cheap and cheerful remote usability tests where volunteers look at websites at a distant location without a researcher present. Reports take a variety of forms including heat maps, scatterplots, written comments, charts showing success/fail/abandonment rates (for tasks attempted), and videos of the screen with an audio commentary by the tester describing what they are doing or thinking.

With remote usability research, the testers use their own computer in their own environment (home, library etc) so the results reflect real, everyday user experiences. Other advantages of remote testing are that it's quick, easy and inexpensive to set up. It's often easier to recruit participants than getting them to a lab or your offices, and there's no problem with people not turning up on the day. It's a more natural situation as it's not normal to have someone sitting beside you when you're using a website. You can test dozens or even hundreds of people at once and you can test more than one website.

On the downside, the scope of the results are limited, participants may be doing it for the wrong reasons, such as being bored or swayed by the small amount of money offered to them, and above all what people say and what they do in real life are often two very different things. It can give you some good 'broad brush' insights, but it's dangerous to rely on it as gospel wisdom.

At the moment the majority of usability tests take place with a researcher present in the physical space, but there are now a huge number of firms offering remote usability tests, and an ever-growing selection of free and paid-for tools that allow you to do it yourself. Prices, methods and services vary hugely, so it's worth looking around to find the one that's going to best suit your needs and your budget.

Acting on the findings

Whatever sort of testing and research you use, do be prepared to use the results. If you're new to testing, start with something small to understand the mechanisms and then move on to bigger projects.

Design your surveys so that the information can be collated and analysed. If you have too many questions, you could end up drowning in data. Arrange a meeting so that everyone in the team can see the usability testing videos or hear the research debrief. Be prepared to hear things that you may not like, and welcome the criticisms, as these are things that are currently holding you back.

Above all, use the findings to make changes and incorporate them into your creative work. Test the new approaches to create a virtuous circle of success with harder working catalogues and websites to bring you more flicks, clicks and sales.

Summary

*Testing is the route to consistently improving all your promotions.
Your customers will always tell you what you need to be doing.*

*The main type of test for both online and offline marketing is the A/B
split test. Test one variable at a time so you know what works – or test
a completely different creative treatment.*

*You can test pretty much anything, but use some common sense
and test the big things first. Good things to test include: offers, target
audience, layout and visuals, price, frequency, timing and copy
including headlines, subject lines and body copy.*

*Supplement your testing with qualitative techniques such as usability
research, questionnaires and focus groups to find out why something
worked (or didn't). Use the findings to help you create catalogues and
websites that sell more.*

9 | **Testing and research**

Credits

Artwork and screen shots for Donald Russell: Reproduced by kind permission of *Ian Morrison* of *Donald Russell*, **www.donaldrussell.com**

Artwork and design for Donald Russell: Reproduced by kind permission of *Clive Miller* of *Symbius Design*, **www.symbius.co.uk**

Artwork for David Nieper: Reproduced by kind permission of *Christopher Nieper*, **www.davidnieper.co.uk**

Artwork for Davy's; Reproduced by kind permission of *James Davy*, **www.davy.co.uk** and *Sian Brooks* of *Spyre Limited*, **www.spyre.ltd.uk**

Artwork for dig-it and Mankind: Reproduced by kind permission of *Tony Adams* of *TA Design*, **www.tadesign.co.uk**

Artwork for Eric Hill: Reproduced by kind permission of *James Johnson-Ferguson*, **www.erichill.co.uk**

Artwork for Laverstoke Park Farm: Reproduced by kind permission of *Jody* and *Clare Scheckter*, **www.laverstokepark.co.uk**

Artwork for Love My Dog: Reproduced by kind permission of *Lilly Shahravesh* **www.lovemydog.co.uk** and *Matt Setchell Creative*, **www.mattsetchell.com**

Artwork for Lyco: Reproduced by kind permission of *Charles Barnett*, **www.lyco.co.uk** & *Neil Summerfield* of *Sixsense Design*, **http://www.sixsensedesign.co.uk/**

Artwork for Muddy Puddles: Reproduced by kind permission and *Ian Simpson* of *Catalogues 4 Business*, **www.catalogues4business.co.uk** and *Susie Cullen*

Artwork for Nothing But Toys: Reproduced by kind permission of *Steve Brady* and *Sian Brooks* of *Spyre Limited*, **www.spyre.ltd.uk**

Artwork for Puchi: Reproduced by kind permission of *Paul Hendrick* of *DJH Advertsing*, **www.djhadvertising.co.uk**

Artwork for Turtle Mats: Reproduced by kind permission of *Susan Leaver* of *The Turtle Mat Company*, **www.turtlemat.co.uk** and *Bite CP Ltd*, **www.bitecp.com**

Cartoons reproduced by kind permission of cartoonist *Robert Duncan*, **www.robertduncan.co.uk**

Category overview opening lines reproduced by kind permission of *Malcolm Tucker*, **http://uk.shop.com**

Order form illustration: Adapted from 'Forms that work: Designing web forms for usability' by *Caroline Jarrett* and *Gerry Gaffney*, by kind permission of Caroline Jarrett.

Photograph of author by *Florence Finburgh*, **www.florencefinburghphotography.com**

Photography in Donald Russell artwork by *Dan Baumann* of *Creative Storm*, **www.creative-storm.co.uk**

Quote from Creating a Profitable Catalog: Reproduced by kind permission of *Jack Schmid*, **www.jschmid.com**

Quotes by *Jakob Nielsen* and heat maps reproduced under the terms of use at **www.useit.com**

Reference to Pindar / Verdict Consulting research "Catalogues are On-trend" by kind permission of *Pindar*, **www.pindar.com**

Reference to research by Mail Media, **Centre www.mmc.co.uk** by kind permission of *Angus Morrison* of *Mail Media Centre*

Screen shot of Bathroom Trade website: Reproduced by kind permission of *Darren Monk*, **www.bathroomtrade.co.uk**

Screen shots of Peter Christian website: Reproduced by kind permission of *Nick Alderton*, **www.peterchristian.co.uk** and *Paul Hendrick* of *DJH Advertsing*, **www.djhadvertising.co.uk**

Templates for 'best practice' websites and catalogues kindly supplied by *Paul Hendrick* of *DJH Advertising*

Resources

Catalogue Exchange - a trade group for direct commerce businesses **www.catalogueexchange.co.uk**

CataloguesCatalogues - a free weekly e-newsletter focused on the direct commerce sector **www.cataloguescatalogues.com**

Catalogue e-Business - a monthly trade journal & website for multi-channel businesses **www.catalog-biz.com**

ECMOD Direct Commerce Awards & Show - the longest running event for the direct commerce sector **www.ecmod360.co.uk**

Acknowledgements

I've often wondered why people have such long lists of thank you's at the end of a book, as I'd always seen writing as a fairly solitary activity. I fondly imagined that the writer simply sits down and the words flow onto the paper. Now, having written one, I know that no book ever gets to print without a huge amount of support from a small army of helpers.

It has taken many years for this book to see the light of day and among the many people who inspired me or gave useful comments on the early ideas were Jackie Boakes, Drayton Bird, Chris Cardell, Pierre Cowlard, Kate Douglas, Tim Lawrence, Caroline Shea, Paula Stainton and some of my Words That Sell team, including Claire Harman, Helen Horrocks, Nicola Kearey and Ali Rasch.

Along the way, many people have been very generous with their advice, including Sarah Cloke, Sandra Deeble, Anna Keeling, Susan Isbister, Marilyn Tuck, Jayne Anthony and my publisher Mindy Gibbins-Klein.

Thank you to everyone who has allowed me to quote them or refer to their work. I am especially grateful not only that you were happy to be included, but also for your wonderful messages of support and encouragement. Thank you also to everyone including my dad, who spent their Christmas reading the manuscript to give me comments and reviews. I also want to say a big thank you to all my clients and colleagues. I have learned so much by working with you over the years. Without you this book would not have been possible.

I owe particular thanks to two people who read early drafts and made invaluable comments that shaped the whole structure and tone of the book, Tessa Fallows and Dan Croxen-John. I was also incredibly lucky to have Michael Inns as my book designer, who really brought the words to life.

Finally, I could not have written the book without some fantastic support at home. Au pairs who have helped make my career possible include Jacqui Kuenzel, Liz Stokes, Yasemin Coruhlu, Bara Svorova and Mischa Havlickova. But the biggest thanks go to my long-suffering family, especially in this last year when my husband took my daughter out so often at weekends that the monkeys at Woburn Safari Park now greet them on first name terms. Paul, James, Hugo and Sacha, thank you so much for your patience and especially for those words of encouragement that meant so much it brought a lump to my throat… "Mum, it's really cool."

Mel Henson

Mel specialises in strategy and copy for websites and catalogues, and heads up the multi-channel copywriting agency Words That Sell (www.wordthatsell.co.uk).

She has written for some of Britain's biggest names in home shopping, including Cotton Traders, David Nieper, Donald Russell, House of Bath and Turtle Mats. Several of her clients, including Aspace, Lyco, Muddy Puddles and Stocksigns, have won national 'Best Catalogue' awards.

Mel also runs copywriting training courses for clients including Bradshaws Direct, Davy's Wine Bars, Kew Gardens and the University of Bedfordshire.

Before turning to copywriting, Mel was an executive in leading London advertising agencies, helping to create TV, press and radio advertising for brands such as Immac (now Veet), Melitta Coffee, Cornetto and Carte D'Or Ice Cream. She also worked at Ogilvy & Mather Direct where she learned the principles of direct marketing.

Mel is a popular speaker at industry events such as ECMOD and the Catalogue Exchange and is on the judging panel for the ECMOD 360 European Catalogue and Website awards. She is also an official Ambassador for Women's Enterprise.

Follow **Flicks & Clicks** on twitter **@flicksandclicks**

Visit **www.wordsthatsell.co.uk** for updates and free downloads

Post a review on **www.amazon.co.uk**

Testimonials

*" I wish a book like this had been available when I started out in
this industry. It would have saved me many costly mistakes and
I might be retired by now. It will be a reference work for years."*

Nick Alderton, Managing Director, Peter Christian

*"Very comprehensive - everything you need to know about selling
off the page, whether catalogue or web."*

Tim Curtis, Managing Director, Lands' End Europe

*"Flicks and Clicks represents the A to Z of how to turn both your website
and your catalogue into sales engines. Mel's insight into topics as diverse
as how to build a powerful online brand and developing a successful
split-testing strategy are invaluable."*

Dan Croxen-John, CEO, Applied Web Analytics

*"An intelligent, no-nonsense and extremely readable guide to the logic of selling
via catalogue and web. Mel Henson combines a passion (and talent) for the written
word with a clear understanding of the relevant business mechanics. Flicks & Clicks
is full of sound advice from someone who really knows what she's talking about."*

Paul Cunningham, Managing Director, Aspace

*"In Clicks and Flicks, Mel Henson shares her very clear understanding
of the essentials of good online and offline creative copy writing, based on her
extensive experiences and knowledge of established direct marketing principles.
It delivers a very enjoyable read, providing guidance to both online and offline
marketers, especially those who struggle with writing
for both print and digital media."*

Martin Harvey FIDM, Managing Director, Marshalls

*"It is terrific to see a new title from a British practitioner which draws upon real
world experience rather than theory. With a 21 year history of bringing expertise to
the catalogue & home shopping sector - via the annual ECMOD Direct Commerce
Show, Catalogue e-Business journal and, more recently, Catalogue Exchange -
I know that this book will prove invaluable. Over the years I have brought US
experts like Amy Africa , Kevin Hillstrom, Don Libey and Ernie Schell to share their
expertise with UK audiences - it is great to see that we now have our own experts
emerging to take this teaching further."*

Jane Revell-Higgins, Founder of ECMOD and Catalogue e-Business journal

Index

Printed in Great Britain by
Amazon.co.uk, Ltd.,
Marston Gate.